WALLABY

THE INSIDER'S GUIDE TO BUYING AND WEARING MEN'S CLOTHES

MAKING THE MAN

ALAN FLUSSER

Photographs by Jane Corbett
Illustrations by Gordon Black

WALLABY

A WALLABY BOOK
Published by SIMON & SCHUSTER
New York

Published by Wallaby Books
A Simon & Schuster Division of
Gulf & Western Corporation
Simon & Schuster Building
1230 Avenue of the Americas
New York, New York 10020
WALLABY and colophon are trademarks
of Simon & Schuster

First Wallaby Books Printing May 1981
10 9 8 7 6 5 4
Manufactured in the United States of America

Library of Congress Cataloging in Publication Data

Flusser, Alan, date.
  Making the man.

  "A Wallaby book."
  1. Men's clothing—Purchasing—Directories.
2. Shopping—Directories. I. Title.
TT495.F55   646'.32   80-27230
ISBN 0-671-79147-8

To my father, whose wonderful esoteric wardrobe first whetted my appetite for French lisle, hand-clocked socks, striped English suspenders and garters, Brooks Brothers button-down shirts and alligator tassel-loafers, and whose memory is never far from mind when in my travels I happen upon some exquisite legacy from his time, an item crafted by artists and altogether elegant.

ACKNOWLEDGMENTS

I want to thank first my brother, Martin, who convinced me to do this book and without whose suggestions, encouragement and editorial help this project would not have been possible. But the writing was only one aspect of this project. The illustrations of Gordon Black, an architect, capture visually what I tried so hard to make clear in my writing. Jane Corbett's desire for perfection in her photographs reflects what I hoped would be the spirit of this book.

Special mention must be made of those men, expert in their field, who read portions of the manuscript and made corrections and provocative suggestions: Many thanks to Dennis Halbrey of Anderson and Sheppard, Mr. Brown of Bowring and Arundel, George Cleaverly and John Cannera of Poulsen & Skone, John Linnitt of Grenson, Irene Stuart of De Casi Fashions, and Dick Jacobsen of R. W. J. Co.

Gene Brissie, my editor, was patient and concerned, and always available for advice and consultation. My agent, Meredith Bernstein, persevered where others would have quit. Finally I want to thank my wife, Marilese, not just for her love and belief in me, but for her real contributions to the book and her insistence on its accessibility for the general reader.

CONTENTS

INTRODUCTION

If you've bought men's clothing with any regularity over the past ten years, chances are your closets now house a substantial collection of unwanted garments. Oversized-collar shirts, thin ties, flared pants and wide-lapeled suits—just to name a few. Styles changed so radically and so often during the 1960's and 1970's that what once might have been considered "hip" or "fashionable" now has only nostalgia value. Sophisticated men concerned about the way they dress would not be caught dead in most of these clothes.

The past two decades have been a period of high energy in the menswear industry. Designers creating "new looks" entered the field in force, producing strikingly different collections each season just as they and others had done for years in the women's field. A once staid industry about which George Frazier, America's greatest men's clothing critic, could write, "There is always so little change," suddenly became a marketplace for new ideas.

In many respects this experimentation had a beneficial effect, liberating both men and the mass manufacturers from the stodginess of their sartorial pasts. But at the same time it convinced the industry that the only way to succeed was through change. So what has happened over the past ten years is likely to continue for the next ten. Men will be presented with a succession of changing styles, only with this difference: suits that were $135 in 1970 are now $275 to $400; shoes that were $35 are now $100; $15 shirts are $50 and $60. The "game" has become serious business. Men have no choice now but to become intelligent consumers. Like women they must learn how to weed through the facile and the ephemeral to find those clothes that will keep them stylishly dressed for more than a season.

Unfortunately there are few places to which men can turn for guidance in these matters. The great men's fashion critics of the past have had no inheritors. The magazines and newspapers which once devoted hundreds of pages each year to advice and discussion of men's clothes have turned their interest elsewhere. And those wonderful old salesmen, who understood tradition and style and whose taste could be counted on, are now practically an extinct species. They have been replaced by inexperienced and inarticulate youngsters who don't even know how to tie a bow tie or explain the difference between a shawl-collared jacket and one with a peaked lapel.

It is this void that *Making the Man* aims to fill. It is meant to be used as a reference, a guide for buying men's clothes. Not just for this season or next season, but for the next ten or even twenty seasons.

The first part of *Making the Man* is a compendium of principles that demonstrate how to find quality and lasting style in the clothes you buy. These are not newfound principles. They are guidelines that have perhaps been obscured in recent times but have directed the buying of all good dressers for the past fifty years.

The second part of the book is a worldwide directory of shops where one can be sure of finding clothes of style and value. It is not an exhaustive survey but rather a selective one. Each of these shops is special in its own way.

For many men shopping for clothes used to be a time of great fun and excitement. Recently, because of the money they have thrown away and are sure they will throw away again, it has become something of a chore. If this book has any aim it is to put the joy back into that once special pleasure. Dressing well gives off a rare kind of confidence and exhilaration. Buying well is half the fun.

I. HOW TO SHOP

1.
TAILORED CLOTHING

Suits

MORE THAN with any other single item of clothing it is in buying a suit that a man must exercise his keenest judgment. Shirts, shoes, ties and socks—each has an important contribution to make to a man's overall attire, but none plays as major a role as the suit. This piece of clothing covers 80 percent of the body and actually defines the general mood and impression of one's appearance.

Yet there is another reason (and to most men it is, and well should be, of equal importance) for purchasing a suit only after extreme deliberation: economics. A well-made ready-to-wear suit today costs more than $250. With the present level of inflation likely to continue, that figure will soon be $350, and not long afterwards it may be as high as $400. It's one thing to make a mistake on a $25 shirt and quite another to relegate a $400 suit to the back of the closet, hoping for the day when such "fashion" finally returns.

A fine quality suit, if properly styled and cared for, should provide the buyer with at least ten years of wear if not more. Even at today's inflated prices the per year cost of such a garment does not seem extravagant for even the most meager budget. How then to buy such a suit?

THE SILHOUETTE

The silhouette is the term the clothing industry uses to describe the cut or shape of a garment. To my mind the silhouette should be the primary consideration in the purchase of any suit. The fabric, the details, even the fit should be secondary concerns. Unfortunately it seems far easier for a man to recognize an interesting detail or fabric than to assess the correct silhouette for his body and personality. And yet it's the silhouette that actually determines the longevity of the suit. If this statement sounds dubious, recall the *Nehru* suit of ten years ago—one, for instance, made in gorgeous Shantung silk—or the so-called *Edwardian* suit in rich cotton velvet. Where are they now? Gone, no doubt, to some theatrical wardrobe office or taking up space at the backs of thousands of closets, doomed by the jazzy eccentricity of their silhouettes.

So when you select a suit don't be taken in by the material or an interesting lining, as appealing as either might seem. Nor should you place

The Sack Suit. This suit model is called "the sack" for the simple reason that it fits like one. Popularized by Brooks Brothers over the last forty years, it is shapeless and unsexy but always respectable.

your faith in the store's fitter. A good tailor can work wonders with most garments, adjusting shoulders and hems to specific proportions and needs. But it would take a veritable genius to remake significantly the cut of a garment, and even then the suit would probably never be quite perfect. Consider first the silhouette.

With perhaps a few exceptions the silhouette most flattering to the majority of men is some version of the British-American natural-shoulder suit. This suit, which has soft, lightly padded shoulders and whose shape follows the general lines of the body, has been the staple of fine dressers for the last forty years. Yet curiously the broad mass of Americans has not followed in step. In the 1950's it adopted the so-called Ivy League suit which, instead of being fitted to the body, was cut with straight lines like a sack. This style, as Tom Wolfe observed in his essay "The Secret Vice," was a special boon to the garment industry, which no doubt did all it could to promote the suit. "This Ivy League look was great for the ready-made manufacturers. They just turned out simple bags and everybody was wearing them."

Then in the late 1960's, with the advent of Carnaby Street and the

The single rear vent is an American convention, functional but offering no help in developing a shapely jacket silhouette. Vents on the sides of the jacket would accentuate the waistline and give a false illusion of height.

The Hour Glass. The most popular American silhouette of the past decade. The jacket has rope shoulders, waspish waist and a full skirt about the hips, wide pocket flaps and lapels. The style can flatter a man's body but because of the exaggeration makes everyone look the same.

The high double vents were supposed to be elegant. Instead they move and open like a swinging door when a man walks.

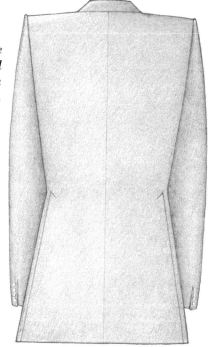

The Wedge. This is the classic European suit with narrow, square shoulders and fitted hips, high armholes and tapered sleeves. On slight-figured Europeans the look is often stylish though very dressy; however, for Americans, this shape is stiff and too confining for our less formal society.

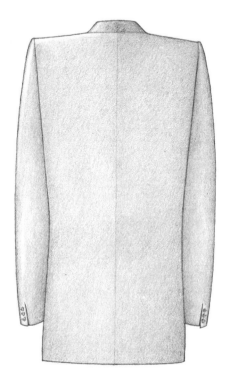

The ventless rear is preferred by most European men today. Unfortunately, it functions poorly as a design. Whenever you want to put your hands in your pockets or sit down, there is no place for the jacket to go. It creases and bunches up in the back.

ensuing men's Peacock Revolution, the popularity of the "sack" suit abruptly waned. Men became increasingly conscious of their physical appearance. They wanted to look young and fit, and the Ivy League suit made most of them appear 20–30 pounds heavier than their actual weight. Unaware of other alternatives, they turned to the greatly publicized Pierre Cardin suit and its various offspring. Cardin offered a sexier look: rope shoulders, waspish waist, full skirt about the hips and fitted low-rise trousers with flared bottoms. This silhouette did indeed make men look taller and thinner, and for almost a decade it reigned supreme in the mass market. But then it too began to lose its appeal, especially among the more sophisticated. These men realized that its effect was too exaggerated, its fat lapels and sharp angles a kind of costume. Indeed, in America this effete, slick-fitting look was directly at odds with the dominating national image of rugged individualism.

But there was another factor at a work as well, perhaps just as important in its demise. This style of body-hugging suit was uncomfortable to wear. While American men were becoming more athletic and active, turning increasingly to sportswear as a mode of dress, these highly stylized suits were fighting their progress each step of the way. Tapered about the chest and waist with high tight armholes, these trusslike garments were not meant for stretching in or even sitting in. When wearing such a suit one did his best to stand immobile like some mannequin in a shop window.

While these monumental changes were occurring in the suit mass market, a small group continued to defy "fashion" by wearing and looking stylish in what it had been wearing for many years. It managed to do this by patronizing custom tailors, most of whose establishments had been operating since before the last world war. Recently its look has been rediscovered by a group of new designers. Of course this discovery is hardly a revelation to those aware of the history of the British-American soft-shoulder suit. This suit actually came to the United States in the 1930's and was called the English Drape. Originating on Savile Row, the Drape model, according to the Seventy-Fifth Anniversary Report of *Men's Wear Magazine*, "had broader shoulders, 'breaks' on either side of its full chest and at the 'blades,' with a definitely nipped-in waist at the front and sides. Its high-rise deeply double-pleated trousers were cut full with a bit of taper toward the cuff."

This silhouette has been with us in somewhat different form since then and has been the mainstay of fine dressers. Only in recent years has its soft classical design been overshadowed by the publicity of the "new," leading men away from an elegant, durable style.

Unfortunately, if history is any guide, this cycle is likely to occur again. Some new exaggerated design will grab the media headlines and if men haven't learned the lesson of the seventies, they will once again be buying suits destined to go out of fashion quicker than the newest diet fad. On the other hand, one can trust the longevity of the well-cut British-Amer-

The British–American Classic. This silhouette has been the staple of fine dressers since the 1930's. Originating on Savile Row, it was brought to notice in America by the visits of the Duke of Windsor and later by the movies of Fred Astaire. The lines of the suit follow those of the body. The shoulders are naturally shaped with only slight padding. There is a definite waist, but the construction is soft so that the cloth can move and adapt itself to each individual body.

British-style side-venting allows for movement but the shorter vents produce a subtlety of look.

ican soft-shoulder suit. Its silhouette follows the natural lines of the body. As long as those lines don't change, men can count on the continued appropriateness of the style and shape.

The suit of a good dresser should reflect no one else's image but his own. This might have sounded obvious in the days when most men's suits were made individually at the local tailor or haberdasher. But ever since suits began to be mass manufactured, the garment industry has tried to create one suit silhouette that would fit all men. At least the sack suit of the 1950's permitted some flexibility. But the designer suits of the past ten years have been so rigid, overpadded and stiffly constructed that every man wearing one ended up looking like everyone else. They looked just like Pierre Cardin or Yves St. Laurent thought they should look. It didn't matter whether they lived in New York or Des Moines, worked in a bank or in an advertising agency. Their image in these high-styled suits was the same.

Any suit a man purchases ought to be flexible enough so that it can reflect him as an individual. Instead of the suit wearing him, instead of him fitting into its mold, it should follow the wearer's lead. This means the construction must not be so stiff as to inhibit the jacket from molding to the wearer's body. There is a strongly held belief at Anderson & Sheppard of Savile Row, one of the finest custom tailors in the world, that if a customer leaves the shop and is recognized as wearing a new suit, it has failed in its job. What the tailors mean is that the suit they have created stands too far apart from the man wearing it, calling attention to itself. Their suits have a minimum of padding in the shoulders and the chest is soft enough so that it can form around the body. This is the kind of softness one should be looking for in a suit.

In the same respect that a stiff, highly stylized suit sharply distinguishes itself from the wearer, so too does any one detail out of proportion to the total design. A misplaced pocket or an overly large lapel will immediately catch a viewer's eye, again creating distance between wearer and garment. Recently we have seen the manufacture of suit jackets with exceedingly narrow lapels. The presence of such lapels forces a man to wear shirts with shorter collars which in turn require skinny ties that make a tiny knot. While all this may be interesting as a change of pace, it's an effect and like all effects will eventually lose viewer interest. At some point it will merely be perceived as a dated oddity. Hardly the future one would choose for a $400 suit.

The lapel of a well-styled suit should extend to just a fraction less than the halfway mark between collar and shoulder line. This creates a proper balance between the lapel and other parts of the jacket, thus honoring the main principle of fine classic tailoring, which is that no part, no detail, should have greater effect than the whole, than the total image of the suit.

The shoulders of this classic suit should be soft, similar in shape to the

The lapel of a well-styled suit should extend to just a fraction less than the halfway mark between collar and shoulder line. The lapel in the illustration, upper left, is too narrow; the lapel in the upper right illustration, too wide. The lapel must be in proper balance with other parts of the jacket.

man's shoulders they sit on. Of course, if a man's shoulders slope sharply away, a little padding could be used to give him a better, healthier look. The jacket itself should follow the taper of the body from chest to waist. The suppression of waist should not be too forced, however, or it will constrict movement.

The armholes of the jacket must be as high as a man can wear them without being uncomfortable. In other words the jacket should fit more like a shirt around the shoulder and arm. This will actually give more flexibility since a large armhole, cut below the meeting of the arm to the shoulder, tends to restrict the arm's movement. From the armhole the sleeve should taper gently to the wrist. This should not be so sharp a taper that it constricts the movement of the arm. But it should clearly indicate the natural narrowing that occurs.

Finally, in choosing your own suit, be sure to look for a model where the jacket is cut slightly on the short side. The idea is to emphasize as long a leg as possible. This makes a man appear much taller. Of course the jacket must be long enough to cover the curvature of the rear. And it should button slightly below or on the natural waist of the man wearing it, never above. This waist buttoning emphasizes the length of the lapel, balancing the shortness of the jacket.

As for the trousers, they too should follow the natural contours of the body, tapering slowly from waist to ankle. With a waist of 30–34 inches, the trousers should have legs with circumferences of 21–22 inches at the knees and 18–19½ inches at the bottoms. Such a description obviously eliminates all types of bell-, flair- and straight-bottom trousers. These styles, which run counter to the natural lines of the body, call attention to themselves, often cutting the wearer at the knees. This is especially damaging to someone of small stature, who ends up looking even shorter.

The popularity of jeans and European-styled pants accustomed men to wearing trousers on their hips. But suit trousers actually look and hang far better when balanced on the waist. Every man, no matter how thin, has a slight bulge in his stomach area. When trousers are worn on the waist they pass smoothly over this bulge in an even drape. Furthermore waist-worn trousers emphasize the smallness of the waist. They sit there comfortably, supported by the hips. Trousers worn on the hip, on the other hand, must be belted tightly for there is nothing to hold them up. In consort with a vested suit, trousers on the hip can only detract from the overall appearance, particularly when there is a gap between vest and trouser top. There is nothing more unsightly (and nothing that draws more attention to the waist) than to have a visible bunch of shirt or belt sticking out from between the vest and trousers. The solution is to reaccustom yourself to the way men used to wear trousers. It made sense then and it still does now.

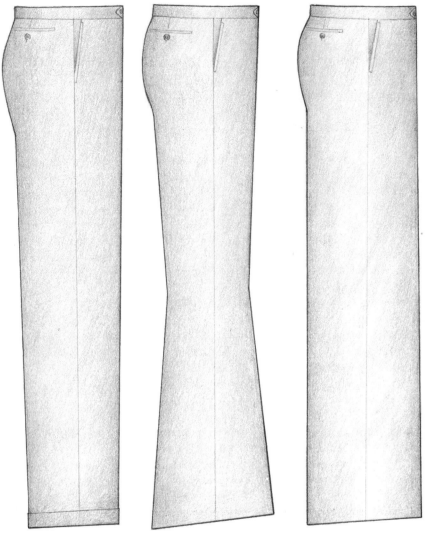

The trouser on the left is tapered. Finished at the bottom with a cuff, it offers a man the most elegant silhouette. Its elegance stems from the simplicity of the line. The trouser is able to follow the shape of the leg with no surprise, no designer details. The cuff is important because it has weight, thus pulling the trouser leg down and allowing it to retain its natural line. The flare-bottomed trousers in the center illustration are designed completely counter to the natural lines of the body. The flare detail calls immediate attention to itself and will interrupt the smooth line of any suit. It has the further effect of cutting a man at the knees, making a short man appear even shorter. Furthermore, even a good-looking shoe will be diminished by the effect of a wide bottom. The straight-leg trouser on the right is the most popular style today, but it is a compromise. The same principle applies to this leg shape as to the full flair except on a smaller scale. It does not follow the natural shape of the body, thus the bottom tends to look sloppy and unfinished.

FIT

The correct fitting of a suit is essential to the achievement of the proper silhouette. Simple tailoring cannot significantly alter a suit's design, but improper fitting can do enough damage to the overall appearance to negate all one's efforts in having made the appropriate selection.

It is often a good idea when shopping for a suit to wear the finest suit you own. This will give the salesman as well as the fitter an introduction to your particular taste. Try also to wear a tie and shirt that will be compatible with the type and pattern of suit you plan on purchasing. Finally, when the suit is being fitted, make sure you have placed in the pockets all those items— a wallet, cigarettes—that you would normally carry.

Once you have selected a suit, examine first the area around the shoulders and neck. At least 50 percent of the suits men wear today do not fit them properly here. The jacket should lie flat on the shoulders without buckles or creases. The lapels should hug the chest while the collar curves smoothly around the back of the neck. If the shoulders are tight or binding, try the next larger size. Suit shoulders cannot be made larger by alterations. If the jacket collar and lapel stand away from the neck, either the manufacturer was careless in attaching the collar to the jacket or the pattern of the jacket is not appropriate to your particular physique. Occasionally this can be remedied by re-attaching the collar but in most instances the problem remains. So if you do authorize the store's tailor to make the attempt, be certain you try the suit on in the store after the alterations are complete. If the collar is still not smooth around the neck, refuse to accept the suit. There is nothing that can destroy the clean lines of a well-tailored jacket more than a collar bouncing on the neck. Instead of allowing the jacket to become a natural extension of the body, the bunching collar makes clear its incompatibility.

Once you find the shoulders and neck satisfactory, continue your inspection downwards. The jacket is not supposed to fit like a glove (leave that to the gloves), but it should make references to the healthy body underneath. This means that the waist is slightly suppressed and the chest and back are large enough to move comfortably in—though not so large that there are sloppy folds. The tailor can usually adjust the waist to your liking, but be careful not to have it taken in so tightly that the silhouette becomes exaggerated and your movements constricted. Also be aware of the effect such a narrowing of the waist can have on the skirt of the jacket. Often a great suppression of the waist will make the jacket spread around the hips, opening the vent or vents in the rear. These vents should never be pulled apart, allowing the seat of your trousers to show. Rather, the vents should fall in a natural line perpendicular to the ground.

As for its length, the jacket should hang just far enough to cover the curvature of the buttocks. You can sometimes have a jacket shortened by a good tailor, but you always take the risk of ending up with the pockets sitting too close to the bottom hem. Such alterations are generally quite expensive.

Curiously one of the most important aspects of a suit's alterations is the least complicated to effect, and yet more often than not it is carried out incorrectly. I'm speaking here about the length of the sleeves. Most men in America wear their jacket sleeves too long and this actually makes them appear dowdy. Indeed, if a costume designer wants a stage actor to appear shabby or down-and-out, he will purposely cut the sleeves too long. On Savile Row a man wearing too long a sleeve is said to be "overcoated."

There's nothing tricky about finding the correct length of the sleeve. All that business of measuring up from the thumb a prescribed number of inches is a waste of time and quite often erroneous. Men's thumbs are known to differ in length. Merely let your arms hang down naturally. Then have the sleeves shortened (or lengthened) to the point where the wrist and the hand meet. The one-half inch of shirt cuff that should show below the sleeve will now never end up in your soup.

When having your trousers fitted, remember first that they should be worn on the waist. Good suit trousers have always been cut this way. That is why if you buy a fine suit and try to wear the trousers on the hips, the crotch will hang too low and look sloppy. Moreover the curvature of the hips will tend to spread the pockets. This will push them out rather than permit them to lie flat, adding inches to your girth.

Once you have the trousers on the waist, make certain the seat and

The sleeve of the jacket should extend no lower than the bottom of the wrist (right). Any longer and a man begins to look dowdy. The shirt sleeve should extend just below the wrist. Fine dressers want to show about one-half inch of linen.

crotch closely follow your own particular contours. Like the armhole of the jacket, the crotch of the trouser should fit as high as is comfortable. This is especially important for giving a clean fit while reducing the length of the long front line from waist to crotch. Such adjustments can usually be made by the store tailor without undue difficulty. But don't have the trousers made so tight that they constrict your movement or limit your comfort.

Altering the shape of the trouser leg is something else again. A 2-inch drop in measurement from the knee to the cuff will give a straight leg appearance. Yet in order for the trouser to follow the natural shape of the body, tapering slightly as I have been recommending, the difference must be at least 2½ inches. Thus: 21–22 inches at the knee, 18½–19½ inches at the cuff. Traditionally the width of the bottom of a man's trouser was cut to balance the size of his shoe. This is a relationship you should still consider, especially if you have a very large foot. In that case a slightly larger bottom might look better. The measurements above are recommended for men with waist sizes 32–36 inches.

If the trouser legs are not cut to your liking, ask the tailor to make adjustments. If he says he can't, maybe you'd do better finding another suit.

When Abe Lincoln was asked how long a man's legs should be, he answered glibly, "long enough to reach the ground." Such advice, somewhat modified, might be used to answer the question regarding the length of a man's trousers. All trousers should be worn long enough to reach a man's shoes. Unlike the sleeves, there is some leeway here. But be careful about the extremes. Too big a break on the shoes begins to have a shortening effect on the length of a man's legs—especially unflattering for short and heavy men. Exposing too much sock can have the same effect. If you have to choose, have the trousers altered on the long side rather than the short. That's the way the British wear them. The slight breaking of the trousers on the shoes brings the eyes down and gives a longer look to the legs.

MATERIAL

There is only one immutable principle governing the selection of suit material. The cloth must be made from natural fibers. This means some type of woven wool in the cooler periods of the year—worsted, flannel, gabardine, etc.—and in the summer, if not a tropical wool, then linen, cotton or silk. Synthetic fibers made from polyester or acrylic are just not substitutable. Without trying to sound arrogant, I believe there is absolutely no way a man can ever be considered well dressed wearing a polyester suit. These fabrics stand away from the body, stiffly retaining their own shape rather than settling on the individual wearer. No matter how hard you try, your suit will somehow always look artificial.

As we all know, natural materials are very expensive today. High-quality wool suiting costing $15 a yard will make a final retail suit cost approximately $350. Cashmere and silk are even more expensive. Yet there are some compensations for the inflationary prices you are forced to spend on traditional suiting fabrics, compensations independent of aesthetic value. Suits of natural fiber wear well. There is no reason a good wool suit should last fewer than seven to ten years. And if you have purchased it in a classical silhouette, no reason why you shouldn't enjoy wearing it that long. Calculated on a per annum basis, even the cost of a $400 suit comes out to less than $40 a year.

There will probably be less maintenance on a natural fiber suit. A fine wool suit rarely has to be dry cleaned. Because air can pass through it, the wool can "breathe" and damp odor from perspiration will readily evaporate. Wool yarn also has the property of returning to its original shape. After a day's wear if the trousers are hung from the cuff and the jacket is hung on a properly curved hanger, the suit will return to its original uncreased form by the following day. Add up the dollars spent in a year of dry cleaning and you have another convincing reason for opting for pure wool.

Perhaps the most important compensation of wearing natural fiber suits is the comfort you can enjoy in having a fabric next to the skin that somewhat simulates its properties. Natural materials have a soft, luxurious feeling. They act like a second skin, letting out perspiration and body heat when necessary, holding in warmth when it's cold outside.

Synthetic fabrics, on the other hand, are like a form of plastic. They have no ability to "breathe." In the summer these suits are hot, holding in the warmth of the body. In the winter they offer no protection from the cold. You can buy a suit with 3–5 percent nylon reinforcement, but any larger amount of synthetic fiber will undermine the natural material's beneficial properties.

The weight of suit material will naturally vary from summer to winter. In the warm months you should look for a tropical weight wool fabric of perhaps 7–9 ounces a yard. In the winter the ideal fabric weight is some-

Wool fibers are naturally resilient. After dry cleaning they become battered and flattened out and need to recuperate, to regain their natural elasticity.

where between 11–13.5 ounces a yard. Any good salesman should be able to tell you the weight of a suit's fabric. Any lighter fabric than that weight will not allow the suit to drape properly. Any heavier than 13.5 ounces will make the suit begin to look bulky and feel too warm indoors.

Much has been said in recent years to encourage men to broaden the color range of their wardrobes. For those men who alternated a blue suit with a gray one, white shirt and blue-and-white tie, this advice was helpful and long overdue. But for others it acted as a kind of trap set mostly by the clothing industry bent on persuading men to buy this year's color, which next year was certain to be replaced by a new "in" color. As the goal of this book is to show men how to insure the longevity of their wardrobes, my suggestions may appear somewhat conservative. But there is plenty of room for color elsewhere in one's attire than in the suit where a whim for this year's rage may mean discarding $400 worth of merchandise the following year.

For most men I would suggest the purchase of suits in the blue or gray range. This might mean gray flannel suits, single- or double-breasted in medium or dark gray; small patterned Prince-of-Wales plaids; pin stripes or chalk stripes on blue or gray backgrounds. In addition I would recommend a single-breasted three-piece tan wool gabardine suit, as well as a double-breasted navy gabardine. Gabardine always looks handsome and can be worn ten months of the year. The best gabardine fabrics come from Italy. Like gray flannel they offer great adaptability, perfect for most occasions, and wearable with almost any color accessories.

In summer you can be more colorful. Wear a blue or gray oxford-striped seersucker or a cotton poplin suit in light beige or khaki. Tropical wool suits in gray pin stripes or glen plaids are also handsome though perhaps less interesting. For the ultimate in comfort and elegance there is nothing to compare with a silk suit, in tan, navy, gray or cream.

These are the basic suitings of any wardrobe. If cut properly, they should flatter almost any man. I have purposely not mentioned brown, green or bright plaid fabrics even though there are some wonderful suitings in these materials. The problem is that many men simply do not look well in them. A plaid suit with a predominantly horizontal pattern will make a short, stocky man appear more so. Vertically striped suits will have the opposite effect. On certain men brown and green are truly unflattering. Charles Revson once said, "A man who wears a brown suit looks like shit." This isn't necessarily true, but if you work for many corporate execs, you'd probably do best sticking to blue or gray. These colors undoubtedly give a man a more formal, more elegant look.

These recommendations on my part are not meant to stifle anyone's attempts to express his own personality or individual nature. I am only trying to make clear that when you leave the classic suitings for more unusual patterns, you are presenting yourself with a more difficult task. Still, this doesn't mean you can't succeed, that you can't find a unique green or brown suit that continues to render service and enjoyment for many years to come. Indeed, it probably is worth the extra effort. But make that extra effort; don't select on whim alone.

DETAILS

These are the finer points. Unless you are patronizing a custom tailor, you may not be able to buy a suit that includes all the following specifications. On the other hand, some of my recommendations (which others might consider less recommendations than personal quirks) may not completely appeal to you. In most cases, however, their presence or absence is a good indicator of the quality or the level of style of the suit in question.

Handwork
The more pieces of a suit that are sewn together by hand the better the quality and, naturally, the higher the price. Industrial technology today allows clothing companies to make a suit almost entirely by machine, but a fine quality manufacturer will still insist on using some handwork. Two areas are particularly significant, and you should check them before buying a suit. First look under the collar. As was previously discussed, the fit of the collar around the neck is crucial, and the collar's attachment to the jacket is not a simple matter. Its curved line requires the contouring of the material as each section is sewn. That's why a top quality manufacturer will insist that the collar be attached to the jacket by hand.

The other important detail involves the setting of the sleeves to the jacket body. If they have been felled by hand, you can count on good fit and proper shape. This is the area that receives the most wear and pressure so a strong binding is also extremely important.

Hand stitching on the edge of the lapel is another detail one might look for. This stitching has no utilitarian value, but it is a nice finishing touch to a lapel and is evidence of a concern for quality on the part of the manufacturer.

Lining
A lovely trapping of fine tailoring is handsome lining. Traditionally (and this is still occasionally available) the body lining was color-coordinated with the suit fabric while striped linings were used in the sleeves. But the color is less important than the quality of the fabric. Make certain it is soft and neatly sewn into the coat.

Curiously, it is actually more expensive to make a suit without a lining than one with a lining. In an unlined jacket all the inside seams must be perfectly finished. Yet when manufacturers in an effort to make clothing softer tried to market unlined jackets recently, Americans refused to buy them. They felt these "unconstructed" jackets must be of lesser quality, or else they just preferred the ease of sliding into their clothing. At any rate there will probably be very little tailored clothing without linings in the future, a trend not necessarily worth mourning. A lining, after all, provides a jacket with increased durability as well as helping to maintain its line.

Buttonholes

The buttonholes are another index to a suit's quality. Examine them carefully. They should be well finished with no threads hanging. If a manufacturer would release a suit with one of its most visible aspects in disrepair, think how little care must have been given to those parts of the suit that don't show.

Real buttonholes on the sleeve, ones that actually work, have long been a symbol of custom tailoring. Mass manufacturers could not employ this detail because stores needed the capability to alter sleeve lengths to fit different size arms. Originally these open buttonholes might have served some real function such as allowing a man to turn back the sleeves while working, or for use with detachable-cuff shirts. But today they are just a symbol. Their presence does not guarantee good tailoring or good styling. And if someone really wants sleeve buttonholes that work, he can have them cut into a suit bought off the rack.

Whether they are working or not, buttons should be on the sleeves of jackets; four each on suit jackets and overcoats; two, three or four on sportjackets. These buttons should be set closely together, their edges barely touching.

The one working buttonhole I do think worth having is on the lapel. After all, it is the most visible of all the buttonholes. Besides, a working buttonhole allows you to sport a flower in the lapel, which from time to time can be a wonderful aid to a stylish look. And on those occasions when you must wear a flower there is nothing considered more outré than the stem being pinned to the lapel. No fine suit lacks a functioning lapel buttonhole.

Pockets

The most important concern regarding pockets should be their relationship to the rest of the jacket. Patch pockets are fine on sportjackets or sporty suits, but for an elegant suit a flap pocket or a besom pocket is more appropriate. (Personally I prefer the flap pocket, which is the one normally found on most American and English suits.) The flaps on the pockets should be consistent with the size of the lapels, neither too large nor too small. Like the lapels they should not draw particular attention to themselves.

Vents

American suits are generally center-vented; British, side-vented; European, non-vented. Given the choice I will always take the British-type side venting. Non-vented suits really make no sense unless you are strolling along the Via Veneto, because as soon as you want to put your hands in your pockets or sit down, there is no place for the jacket to go. It just creases and bunches up on the back until at the end of a few hours it looks as if you've been wearing the suit for a week.

The American single vent gives no help in developing the suit silhouette. It does not emphasize the lines of the body, but instead acts strictly as a functional detail. In a sense it is a compromise on the British version, allowing the manufacturers to eliminate one or two extra steps in the manufactuing process. (If you can cut one slit instead of two, why make extra work?) British side vents, on the other hand, give the jacket a little extra movement and fluidity. But make certain the vents are cut no higher than 8 inches. When the side vents are too high they become exaggerated in appearance, and what was supposed to be elegant has suddenly become a kind of swinging door.

Trouser Tops

There are two styles of trouser tops, pleated and plain front. Plain-front trousers give a trimmer look, but they are somewhat restricting on the movement of the body. Trousers were originally made with pleats and for good reason. When a man sits down his hips and buttocks spread. Trousers designed for comfort, then, would be made with extra material around the hips or with some device capable of keeping pants snug when one is standing but allowing them to spread when one sits—hence, the pleat.

You don't need an accordion of five or six pleats to control the material. One deep pleat on each side of the center zipper, then one narrow pleat farther to each side are enough. These pleats should be turned inward toward the fly, directing the eye toward the middle of the body to give a trimmer look.

The trouser pockets can either be sewn on the side seams or cut slightly on a slant, a style that is referred to as "quarter top." The quarter tops make more sense if your trousers have no pleats because they will break up the wideness of the trousers across the hips. Whichever you choose, though, the facing inside the pockets should be deep enough so that one does not notice the cotton lining even sitting, when the pockets have spread open.

Trouser Bottoms

There is no hard-and-fast rule for the finishing of trouser bottoms. There are fine dressers who wear cuffs and those who don't. It was the British landed gentry who actually invented cuffs. In the days when trousers were

The pleats on properly fitting trousers should not be pulled open across the front. They should lie flat across the abdomen.

If pants fit properly there should be no pulling across the pockets either. The pockets should always sit flat on your sides. A pocket that pulls open means the pants fit too tight. It is important that there is enough facing lining the pocket so that if you sit down the lining does not show.

made only with straight bottoms, country squires would turn up their pants' legs when they went out hunting or watching their horses race in order to protect the material. Today, cuffs in England are still referred to as "turn-ups."

Cuffs are heavier than plain bottoms and pull the pants down snugly on the shoes. And because they are a kind of edging, cuffs seem to me to give a more finished look to the suit. They should be worn 1½–1¾ inches wide, depending on the height of the man, and should hang parallel to the ground.

It is generally not advisable to wear cuffs with straightleg trousers. The thickness of the cuffs would draw too much attention to the already wide bottoms. If you don't wear cuffs, the trouser bottoms should have a slight angle, the trouser length 1–1½ inches longer in back than front.

Vests

In the last few years 70–80 percent of men's suits have been sold with vests. This is unlikely to continue in the 1980's, however, because manufacturers have found that the cost of making a vest can hardly be recovered for the additional price they can charge the consumer. Yet if you do have the opportunity to buy a vest with your suit, do so. For a little extra money your suit's wearability can be significantly increased. A vest worn at night makes a suit appear much dressier. During the day at the office you can take off your jacket, and wearing just the vest, feel comfortable yet still look well turned out. There is also something to be said for the warmth a vest adds in the winter. Originally designed to offer extra protection from the wind for those men driving in open carriages, they make just as much sense today, especially as the energy crisis is likely in the near future to induce landlords to lower the temperatures of their buildings even further.

Vests should fit cleanly around the body, covering the waistband of the trousers and just peaking above the waistbutton (or middle button) of the suit jacket. Good vests are often cut so that one doesn't button the bottom button. They are adjustable in the rear and are lined with material that matches the jacket or sleeve linings of the suit. Proper suit vests have four slightly slanted welt pockets, two just below the waist and two breast pockets. The lower pockets can accommodate a watchpiece or eyeglass; the upper pockets, a pen or reading glasses.

When the jacket is buttoned at the waist one should be able to see just a small part of the vest above it. Any higher than this and the effect becomes strained, concealing too much of the tie as well. Of course the entire elegance of the three-piece suit is destroyed if the trousers are worn on the hips below the bottom of the vest. Then the shirt or belt sticks out badly, interrupting the smooth transition of the silhouette.

An easy way to add variety to dressing is to wear an odd vest on occasion. The most beautiful ones are made from lightweight flannel or

Proper suit vests have four slightly slanted welt pockets, two just below the waist and two breast pockets. They are often cut so that you don't button the bottom button.

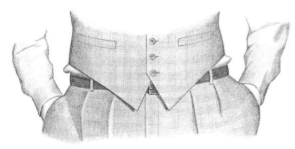

There should be no gap between the bottom of the vest and the top of the trousers. When such a gap does occur (below), it is usually because the trousers are not being worn on the waist. (Many trousers are cut with such a short rise they can only be worn on the hips.) The bottom of the vest must completely cover the waistband of the trousers.

Sport vests can be styled with lower flap pockets.

doeskin—in white, yellow, red or tattersall. A white or pale yellow vest can give a dark suit an added touch of elegance while the red and tattersall vests look best with tweeds. Vests that are worn with sport suits can take a flap pocket on the bottom, a more casual detail.

Sportjackets

THE FIT and styling of a well-cut sportjacket closely follows that of the classic suit jacket. Where the two might differ is in their materials and perhaps in some of the specific detailing. These differences are as much a reflection of their independent origins as well as their present differential roles.

Originally a sportjacket was nothing more than a suit worn with a nonmatching pair of pants. Later, men began to buy jackets to wear with white flannel or odd trousers. This became the outfit of the country elite, or the uniform for a particular sport. Today they are worn in a wide variety of situations—on weekends, at evening get-togethers or at those jobs where an atmosphere of informality is called for. Because of the casual nature of these situations, a freedom of expression is permissible that would be inappropriate to those contexts where suits are generally demanded. Take advantage of this freedom with texture, color or pattern. You might select a nubby tweed fabric in a lovat hue, or a rich red or green cashmere. Or maybe a houndstooth check, a herringbone or a subtle plaid. Sportjacket materials can be on the heavy side for sportjackets are often worn out-of-doors as a kind of outercoat over a sweater.

For true versatility the blue blazer, either single- or double-breasted, is an excellent investment. Depending upon the accessories that accompany it, a blazer can appear as casual as a cardigan sweater or, when worn with matching blue or black buttons, as formal as a dark suit.

In the same way that accessories can affect the appearance of a blazer, detailing on a sportjacket can change its look. Real leather buttons, leather patches on sleeves, welt seams sewn on lapels and patch pockets, collar tabs and ticket pockets can give a wool jacket a most sporty effect—the perfect garment in which to watch a fall afternoon football game or relax before a winter's fire. For the most elegant "in-town" look, one must avoid the sporty frills. Clean flap pockets, edge-stitched seams and bone or matching buttons are the appropriate details for this attire.

When considering the purchase of a sportcoat try to imagine how it will look after five years of wear, slightly roughed up and worn. If you think it's the kind of old friend you'd like to have around, then buy it.

Overcoats

THE BASIC principles of silhouette, fit and material that guide one in buying a classic suit should be followed in the purchase of an overcoat. As in the suit jacket, the shape of the collar around the neck is the key area of fit. The collar should lie flat and curve smoothly around the neck, not ride up.

When you try on an overcoat, make sure you are wearing a jacket underneath. There should always be enough room for a jacket or sweater (with no feeling that you are being bound) since in most cases that is what you'll be wearing underneath. Sleeves should be fitted slightly longer than the jacket sleeve, ½ inch below the wrist. No shirt linen or jacket sleeve should be visible.

Where most men err in fitting their overcoats is in the length. The bottom of the coat should fall just below the knees, or if you prefer a longer overcoat, then 6 or 8 inches below the knees. This length is crucial. When overcoats are above the knee, a man looks bulky and stunted. Because the upper part of the body is massive compared to the rest, and because this massiveness is accentuated even further by the wearing of a jacket covered by an overcoat, the length of the coat is needed to rebalance the body's proportions.

A well-fitting overcoat hangs anywhere from 2–3 inches below the knees. Because the upper part of the body is massive compared to the rest, the length of the coat is needed to rebalance the body's proportions.

The rear vent on an overcoat should never extend higher than the bottom curvature of the buttocks. Not only does a man lose his style when wind blows open the long flaps, but it can be cold and uncomfortable.

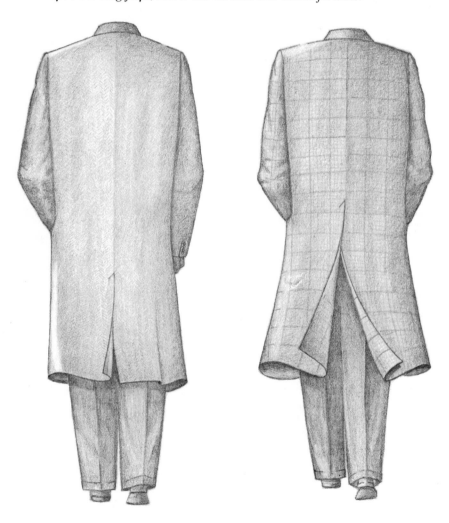

On a pragmatic level long coats offer greater warmth and protection. Why should you have to expose knees and legs to the ice and cold when they can be comfortably enveloped in wool?

In the same practical vein one must wonder about manufacturers who produce overcoats with high rear vents. Not only do you look ridiculous when the wind blows open the long flaps exposing the seat of your pants, but it can be awfully cold and uncomfortable. Rear vents should never extend above the bottom curvature of the buttocks.

There is a plethora of overcoats manufactured today in a wide variety of styles but only a few that can be considered "classic." These are coats which have proved their mettle in the past and are certain to retain their stylishness in the future. For daytime wear this might mean a Harris tweed double-breasted overcoat in a shade of gray or brown; a dark tan covert cloth coat with matching velvet collar; a camel's hair "polo" coat, double-breasted with a belt in the back; or a fawn-colored, double-breasted British warmer. In the evening consider a Chesterfield overcoat of black wool with a black velvet collar or a dark tweed with a velvet or fur collar.

Many of these fine coats come in single- or double-breasted styles. (One should remember that double-breasted coats tend to be warmer because of the second layer of material that crosses the front of the coat.) There are also handsome coats with raglan-shouldered sleeves. However be aware that if you are wearing a square-shouldered jacket underneath, it will stick out under a raglan sleeve, impairing a smooth drape.

Good overcoats are expensive today because of the amount of material they use and because this material is even more costly than fine suitings. Yet since you only wear overcoats to and from places, they really can last a lifetime, especially if the overcoat is made from fine, long-staple wool. Like suits, they are especially durable if they can be given a day's rest between wearings.

It is no easy matter finding a well-styled raincoat today. Manufacturers tend to cut them too short, generally above the knees. The cotton gabardine trench coat is, of course, the classic, but there are fly-fronted coats in cotton or wool gabardine that are equally appropriate. Choose tan rather than dark blue or black.

Proper Care

THE MAIN causes of wear in tailored clothing are the dirt, dust and grit that accumulate in the fabric. Regular brushing, therefore, does much to prolong the life of the garment.

To give the fabric a chance to keep its shape, try not to wear your suit, sportjacket or overcoat for more than one day at a time. When it is not in use, empty the pockets. Then hang it on a solid, shaped and curved wooden hanger. An overcoat or jacket made of soft fabric, such as cashmere or camel's hair, should be steamed occasionally. By hanging it in a bathroom with the hot water running, some of the natural moisture removed by excessive indoor heat can be restored.

When it becomes necessary for your suit or coat to be dry-cleaned, make certain the shop you patronize is reliable. Cheap dry cleaning can ruin the cloth. In any event the dry-cleaning process batters the fibers of the wool yarn. These fibers need time to recuperate, to regain their natural elasticity. When the garment returns from the cleaners, take it immediately out of the plastic bag, shake it so that air can mix with the battered fibers, then hang it up. Let a day or two pass before you wear it. If possible hang your newly cleaned jacket or coat in a garage or wherever there is damp air. Air and moisture is what the wool yarn needs most.

A fine wool garment treated properly will last for years. It will continue to give maximum enjoyment with a minimum amount of care.

2.
DRESS
SHIRTS

WHAT THE silhouette is to the suit, the shirt collar is to the dress shirt. The collar represents the major styling effort of the shirt and is the key factor affecting its long-term wearability. Indeed, when worn with a tie under a suit or sport jacket, the collar and a ½ inch cuff is practically all one ever sees of a dress shirt.

There exists today a wide spectrum of shirt collars—button-down and spread collars; tab, rounded, pinned and wing collars. Each has its various adherents; each can look well under the proper circumstances. Thus unlike for the suit silhouette, there's no reason a man must confine himself to only one style. Still there are some guidelines that should govern collar selection.

Perhaps the most important aspect to consider is the relationship of the shirt collar to one's own physical proportions. Proper balance is what one is seeking. If a man is large with a broad face and bullish neck, nothing will appear sillier under his chin than a tiny collar—rounded, spread or otherwise. Conversely, a high-set collar with 4-inch points will overwhelm a small man with delicate features.

For the average man wearing a standard straight-point collar, the collar points should be no smaller than 2½ inches nor larger than 3¼ inches. A much larger man would do better with a 3½–3¾-inch collar. The proportions of the shirt collar can either draw attention to a man's physical irregularities or de-emphasize them, which is generally the more flattering course to follow. Therefore if you have a short neck, look for shirt collars that lie flat.

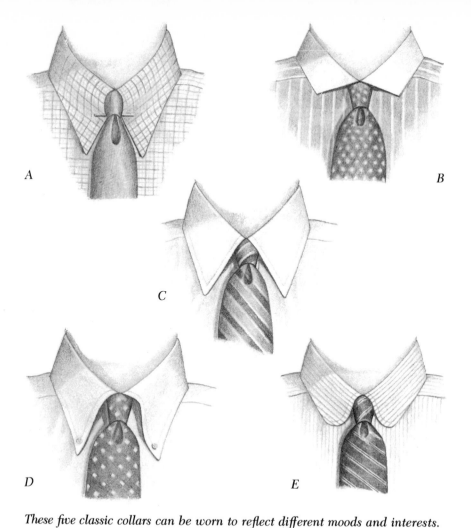

These five classic collars can be worn to reflect different moods and interests. In each, the shape and size of the knot of the tie is in the proper relationship to the length and spread of the collar. Also notice that each tie has a proper dimple made under the center of its knot. Picture a straight line bisecting the V of the collar extending down through the dimple of the knot. This imaginary line is one way you can judge whether your tie and collar are in harmony. When this relationship is executed properly, a subliminal image of authority is projected. A) The pinned collar gives your attire a more formal look. Make sure the collar you pin, however, does not have too wide a spread. The pin itself should be between 1⅝ and 1⅞ inches long. B) The stiff, cutaway collar was popularized by the Duke of Windsor. He used a larger knot of his own invention (the Windsor knot) to fill the wide gap between the edges of the collar. The style is temperamentally English, dressy and dramatic. C) The straight-point collar is simple and correct. It can be worn in daytime or evening, for sport or dress. Its versatility makes it the most popular style worn by men today. D) The button-down collar with a "roll" is soft and sporty. When it was first designed, shirtmakers felt the extra-long points needed buttons to keep them down and out of the way. E) The rounded collar can be worn with or without a pin. It reflects a softer appearance than the straight-pointed collar and can be worn for sport or dress.

If your neck is giraffelike, a higher band collar will tend to shorten its length.

After considering the size of the collar, one should next examine the actual design. The ideal shirt collar forms an upside-down V with the edges of the collar meeting at the throat. No space should be left between the edges. If the shape and width of your tie is appropriate to the shape and size of the shirt collar, no extra space is ever needed. Such collars are difficult to find today except in custom-made shirts because mass manufacturers want their shirts to fit any size tie. One should therefore buy those shirts whose collars have the least tie space between them so that a small elegant knot will not be left in a vacuum between the collar points.

In choosing the proper shirt collar to wear with a specific suit or sportjacket, consider first the image the suit projects. Sportjackets and tweedy suits are informal, casual. Obviously they should not be worn with a high starched collar but rather with a soft button-down or a rounded collar, or even perhaps with a long-pointed collar that can be gathered together with a pin. For dark, more formal attire one should wear a stiffer collar with sharp points—straight or widely spread, like the short cutaway the Duke of Windsor used to sport. Somehow a button-down collar just looks too casual after 6 PM if one is trying to dress for evening.

The shirt collar itself is stitched around the edges to stiffen and hold the folded material in place. In general this stitching should not be more than ¼ inch from the collar's edge. And in dress shirts it should never be obvious. Contrast stitching only acts to destroy the quiet relationship of tie and shirt and can easily appear as an affectation. No stitching at all gives the collar a cheap, mass-produced look.

FIT

The most important consideration in the fit of a shirt is comfort. The neckband should never choke, nor should the body of the shirt bind a man's torso. The neckband should fit snugly so that the collar doesn't fall down the neck. But if it is too tight it will spread the collar creating a larger space where the tie knot sits.

The body of the shirt should have no more material than is necessary to allow a man to sit comfortably. Excess material bulging around the midriff could destroy the lines of the jacket. Yet if you do buy a shirt with too large a body, a seamstress can take in the side seams or put darts in the back to reduce the size. The darts are actually more practical since if you put on weight they can be taken out. The length of the shirt is also an important concern. It should hang at least six inches below the waist so that it stays tucked in when you move around. It should not be so long, however, that it creates bulges in the front of the trousers.

As for the sleeves of the shirt, they should show a good half inch beyond the sleeves of your jacket. If you bend your arm and the cuff recedes behind the wrist, the sleeve is too short. A proper size sleeve will allow you to move your arm in any position without withdrawing the cuff. The cuff itself should fit snugly enough to hold its place on the wrist without appearing as a tight bracelet.

MATERIAL

What is true about suit material is equally true of shirt cloth. The best shirts are made from 100 percent natural fibers. This means primarily cotton. Silk shirts, of course, can be very lovely on first wearings. But their maintenance is a serious drawback. Optimally, silk shirts must be hand-washed, yet most people simply send them to be dry-cleaned. After several such cleanings, they never again feel or look completely clean since the perspiration has not been washed out. If you have the money, you'd be making a better investment if you bought shirts in fine, long-staple cotton. These can be just as elegant as silk and are more comfortable to wear.

Synthetic shirt materials have in recent years received an immense amount of publicity and acclaim. They are durable and resist wrinkling. Many of them can be washed and dried with no need of ironing. But like synthetic suit material, the non-natural-fiber material used in shirts today—a poly-cotton mixture—inhibits the flow of air. Instead of adjusting to the body's temperature these shirts tend to change it, causing excess perspiration and discomfort. In this respect such material can have a more serious effect on body comfort than synthetic suits. After all, a shirt lies directly next to the skin.

It is interesting to note that polyester shirts have never sold well in Europe. This is probably less a matter of comfort than style. No matter how hard the manufacturers have tried, they have been unable to duplicate successfully the feel and look of natural-fiber cloth with synthetic mixtures. There is a sheen to polyester shirts that calls immediate attention to their false constituents. And since the huge jump in oil prices these shirts are no longer the bargains they once were. The chemical base of polyester yarn is composed primarily of petroleum.

The men's Peacock Revolution of the 1960's left a legacy of interest in shirts of all colors, stripes and patterns. Today a wealth of material exists for the shirt buyer and there is absolutely no reason why he shouldn't indulge his every whim. Blue, yellow and pink oxford cloth shirts, for example, have always looked wonderful, particularly with traditional, soft-shouldered clothing. And oxford cloth can be beaten to death without damaging its appearance. For shirts in other colors, try models in end-on-end weaves where the colored yarn is mixed with white. This gives a more interesting texture for a solid colored shirt than broadcloth, which always looks fairly dull. Whatever you do, though, stay away from the flat, strident colored shirts that were all the rage several years ago. They give off too harsh and unsubtle an effect and were always a little slick. If you like patterns, keep them small so that the shirt appears like a solid from a distance. Striped shirts, however, may be bold or muted.

By all means, don't forget that old standby—pure white. In the great flood of color of the last fifteen years, white seems to have received short shrift. Yet on those very special occasions there is nothing more elegant than a starched white shirt in a fine pima cotton, especially when worn with a dark blue or dark gray suit and small-patterned silk tie. Or if you don't care for all white, then perhaps a colored shirt with white color and cuffs. This is a dressy English touch. However make sure your collar is not too large or it will look overpowering against the contrasting background. Choose a cutaway or a shorter round collar.

DETAILS

Cuffs

There are two types of shirt cuffs: the barrel and the French. The barrel cuff fastens with one or two buttons. The French cuff is folded back along the wrist and then closed by means of a cuff link. The French cuff is much more expensive to produce, so naturally manufacturers have lately taken to marketing only the barrel cuff. The French cuff, however, is considerably more elegant. When worn under a dark suit, the double fold of the French cuff combined with the bit of light that is the cuff link adds a richness to a man's attire that a single cuff and button simply cannot duplicate.

The means by which the cuff itself—either barrel or French—has been attached to the sleeve is often a reliable index to the quality level of the shirt's manufacture. This attachment is no simple task. A big sleeve, one that can fit comfortably around the biceps and forearms, must be reduced in circumference and then sewn to a cuff that fits the smaller wrist. Often the sleeve is simply tapered in its shape so that there is little extra fabric to tuck into the cuff. But if instead the sleeve has been carefully folded into several even pleats and then attached to the cuff, it is undoubtedly a shirt that has been made with care. In England the custom shirtmakers actually sew small pleats in a complete circle around the cuff. French shirtmakers use a symmetrical pattern, folding two or three pleats into the cuff on each side.

Monograms

Monograms are a nice way of personalizing your shirt. They are considered a touch of elegance, though not when they are ostentatiously placed

The shirt monogram should give only a subtle identification of the wearer. If your shirt has no pocket, the monogram should be placed 3–5 inches up from the waist, depending on the height of the wearer.

on cuffs or on the collar of a shirt so as to act like billboards. Keep the lettering simple and the initials discreet (no larger than ¼ inch high). Place them approximately 5 or 6 inches up from the waist, centered on the left half of the shirt. If the shirt has a pocket, center the initials on it.

Shirt monograms are usually associated with custom-made shirts, but they can be sewn on any store-bought model. If the store where you buy your shirts doesn't offer the service, check the yellow pages.

Plackets, Yokes and Gauntlets

These three items of obscure terminology can offer further clues to the quality level of a shirt's manufacture.

The placket is that piece of material on the front of the shirt where the buttonholes are placed. It used to be a separate piece of cloth sewn to the front, but now shirtmakers merely fold the edge of the material. All fine dress shirts are made with a placket that is approximately 1½ inches wide. The placket gives the shirt a definite center line and makes a clean finish where the shirt sides join to be buttoned.

The yoke is the strip of material sewn across the shoulders to attach the front and back pieces of the shirt. In former days certain custom shirt-

If your shirt has a pocket, the monogram should be placed in its center.

There is nothing more overstated than to wear a monogram on a shirt cuff or collar.

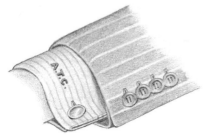

All finely made shirts have a sleeve placket button or, as they say in England, a "gauntlet" button. This button prevents the shirt from opening and showing bare skin.

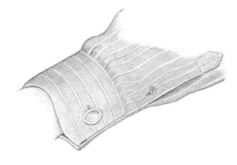

makers used to use a split yoke—two yokes joined in the center—so that they could adjust each shoulder separately. One yoke is actually enough. And in present times that is probably all one can expect. Inexpensive shirts have eliminated even that.

The gauntlet is the English term for the sleeve placket, that open area just before the cuff. A well-made shirt has a working button on the placket so that this gap can be closed. The gauntlet button originated in order to enable men to roll back their cuffs while washing as well as to hold the cuff in place. Obviously a gauntlet button is not one of life's dire necessities, though in certain circles a show of bare wrist is considered in as poor taste as a show of skin between sock and trouser cuff. On the other hand, a buttoning gauntlet does permit a better fit around the forearm and is one more indication of a manufacturer's interest in producing quality apparel.

3.
SHOES

Fashion authorities have long been in agreement that shoes can be the quickest giveaway to a man's style sense and social position. George Frazier, former columnist for *Esquire* magazine and the *Boston Globe*, would often remark, "Wanna know if a guy is well-dressed? Look down." Diana Vreeland, Frazier's counterpart in the women's fashion world, now head of the Metropolitan Museum's Costume Institute, concurs. Speaking of developing a wardrobe, she advises, "First, I'd put money into shoes. No variety, just something I could wear with everything. Marvelous shoes and boots. Whatever it is you wear, I think shoes are terribly important."

Shoes do tell much about the person wearing them. A man who buys fine leather shoes today shows he respects quality, that he has confidence in his taste and in his future. So don't let others judge you wrongly merely because you tried to save a few bucks on your shoes. It is true that buying a fine pair of shoes has become an expensive proposition. Top quality leather skins are in sharp demand; labor costs have skyrocketed. But like other items of quality apparel a well-made pair of shoes will give years of fine service if they are properly cared for. They must be a design, however, that remains stylish throughout the years.

The great-grandson of the legendary English bootmaker, John Lobb,

A properly designed shoe closely follows the natural shape of the foot. The longest part of the foot is the distance from the end of the heel to the big toe. The shape of the well-designed shoe is straight and longer on the inside and shorter and more rounded on the outside. Note that mass-manufactured shoes focus their length on the middle portion of the shoe.

recently published a book about his work entitled *The Last Must Come First.* The last is the wooden form around which a shoe is made, hence, also a reference to the shape of the shoe itself. Lobb's pun, which was directed at the art of custom shoemaking, is actually a good guide for buying ready-made shoes. Examine first the last, or the shape of the shoe.

The shape of a shoe should follow as closely as possible the actual shape of your own foot. The foot is not a particularly attractive feature of the anatomy and a well-styled shoe will work to diminish its ungainliness by making it appear sleeker and smaller. Think of the way a glove fits the hand. There are no excess bulges or gaps. A shoe should be cut similarly: no bulbous toes or crevices in front, a smooth line of leather following closely along the instep down to the edge of the toe. A custom-made shoe is designed to follow the shape of the foot so closely that the outside line and sole is curved (like the foot) while the inside (instead of being symmetrical) follows an almost straight line. A last of this sort in a ready-made shoe is a sign of elegance and knowledge on the part of the manufacturer.

The sole must also work to lighten the effect of the shoe. A heavy welted sole or double soles on a shoe make the foot appear thick and inelegant. The double-soled shoes that many businessmen wear today, either in a heavy grain leather or with wingtip perforations, were marketed after World War II by manufacturers who based their design on Army issue. These shoes seem really more appropriate for storming an enemy village than for strolling along a city street. Look for a shoe with a sole no thicker than ¼ inch. The heels should be low and follow the line of the shoe. They should not be

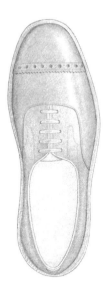

A shorter medallion and a closer welt around the outside of the shoe on the right makes it seem shorter, thinner and sleeker.

A shorter, more elegant look is given the shoe on the right simply by making the vamp shorter.

designed as lifts. Most importantly, both sole and heel should be clipped close to the edge of the shoe with no obvious welt around the outside. The sole's function is simply protection and support. It should not interfere with the shoe's shape or be overly visible.

The vamp, on the other hand, is what one sees most on a shoe. It is the piece of leather that covers the top of the foot. By keeping this piece of leather low on the instep, the front of the shoe will appear shorter, making the entire foot seem smaller. This deaccentuation of length gives the foot a sleeker look. Especially with tapered-bottom trousers, one wants to minimize the boatlike effect of any shoe. Naturally, the vamp should not be cut so low that the shoe can easily fall off. It can, however, come close to resembling a man's slipper.

In sum, a man should look to purchase only those shoes that have a small, well-shaped toe, thin, closely clipped soles and heels and a short vamp. These are the shoes that will give feet the most aesthetically pleasing look.

Traditionally there have been two sources that have supplied America with its better quality shoes—England and Italy. Even so, the products of these two countries differ quite significantly in design. Italian shoes are trim and lightweight. British shoes have a somewhat more substantial appearance. These differences can perhaps be attributed to diverse climates as well as the differing origins of each country's shoe industry.

The Italian ready-to-wear men's shoe industry began as an offshoot to the women's industry. It brought with it an interest in lightness and softness, criteria that have always ruled the women's market. The fine calf skin uppers are glued to the leather soles with no weltings and no inner soles to encumber the sleek look. They are made almost completely by hand with a craftsmanship and finesse that is unequalled elsewhere.

The modern British men's shoe industry came into its own immediately following the end of World War I, those companies having lost their Army boot contracts turning to the commercial marketplace. The qualities of strength and durability which made their boots legendary during the war were now directed toward shoes for the consumer. Unlike people in Italy, where the climate is generally dry and warm (except in Milan), the English have always had to contend with the worst elements of rain and cold. Their shoes were thus constructed of heavier skin which was not glued to the sole but sewn with a leather welt. British manufacturers, moreover, inserted a second leather sole—a middle sole between the outer sole and the inner—to make the shoes even more durable.

All of this interest in protection and durability gives the British shoe and its American offspring a fuller, more solid look. And yet I must confess I do prefer it to the Italian shoe. Italian shoes have always seemed to me not quite masculine enough in their appearance. Paired with a nubby tweed suit or even a fine flannel, they seem almost dainty, without any of the solidity one might expect (or want) to support a man's foot. There is no doubt that the shoes in Italy are more creatively made, and yet the balance is just not right for the classic look we have been delineating.

Furthermore Americans must contend with climatic conditions that rival England's. And Italian shoes, though they can look marvelous on a sunny day, literally fall to pieces in rain or snow. Within moments of walking on a damp street one can begin to feel moisture creeping into one's shoes. They are pleasant enough to stroll in, but definitely not advisable for use in long walks. They offer little support or protection, and only under rare circumstances will they last five years.

In selecting shoes for a durable, long-term wardrobe, shoes that are certain to be stylish for many years to come, I would seek first black or brown English-styled brogues with plain fronts or medallion toe caps. Either one is a good, all-purpose shoe, appropriate for business or less formal after-five activity. Make certain, however, that the sole is clipped close to the edge of the leather upper.

A brown or black tassel loafer of English design is another fine all-purpose shoe. The brown tassel looks particularly well with sportjacket and trousers, but don't be unnecessarily cowed by the old dictum that says only black shoes should be worn with dark suits. For years now many Americans, particularly New Englanders, have been wearing high-polished brown shoes with dark suits. They can look marvelous together and it is now a combination that has become accepted almost everywhere except perhaps in England where the traditionalists still hold sway. There, for a more elegant look, the men match a dark suit with a pair of brown suede shoes. This too is a handsome look.

In the summer, for a more colorful feeling there is nothing like a brown-and-white or black-and-white bloucher or slip-on. Unfortunately most of these being made today use a synthetic substitute for the white instead of the traditional buckskin. These I would shy away from, as I would from most two-tone shoes. The chances of finding a classy one are infinitesimally small. For great summer sportwear, the white buck tassel loafer is a perennial favorite.

FIT

Ever since the government banned the use of X-ray machines, fitting a pair of shoes has become strictly a matter of feel. There are no real secrets in this regard. The size that's comfortable for you is the size to buy. However most men's feet are slightly different sizes. If that is the case always buy the shoe to fit the larger foot. Remember, though, that certain soft leathers, particularly in loafers, will stretch up to a half-size. A good fit should allow you to wiggle your toes while the heel fits snugly into the back of the shoe. There should be good support underneath the instep.

CARE

The best way to care for a pair of leather shoes is to keep them polished and to give them ample rest. Polish protects the leather from water and from scuffing. Many men buy new shoes and are so eager to wear them that they forget to rub on a first coat of polish. Before they know it they have put a scuff in the leather that is there for life, or they have allowed the skin to dry out. A heavy douse of water on unprotected leather can weaken the strength of the delicate upper skin. All of these eventualities can be protected against with a good coat of saddle soap or shoe polish. (Saddle soap will clean leather and keep it supple. However for a bright luster, you must use polish afterwards.)

Leather absorbs moisture. This is what allows it to stretch and why it is so important for shoes to be given time to rest. Never wear a pair of leather shoes for more than one day at a time. Leather breathes like cotton or wool. It needs at least a day or two to dry out, to release trapped moisture and return to its original shape. By alternating the shoes you wear, and keeping shoe trees in them, there is no limit on the years they will last. Worn day after day, the skin becomes moldy and attenuated until finally the suppleness disappears and the leather begins to crack. Leather is a skin. Treat it with the respect and care you give your own.

DETAILS

Skins

It is the skin used in constructing the upper part of the shoe that more than any other factor determines the price level of the shoe. The real difference between a $50 shoe and a $150 shoe is in the quality of the leather. Shoes today are made from kid skin, calf skin, cow hide or suede. More exotic leathers such as alligator have been banned in the United States though lizard and ostrich are still available.

The softer, more supple the leather, the higher the quality. Supple leather will last longer as it does not easily crack. Its lighter appearance makes a shoe more elegant. Such leather generally comes from smaller animals, kids and calves, which means there is less of it, hence its higher price. Before you purchase a high-priced shoe, feel the leather. Bend the shoe and watch how the leather moves. It should be soft and flexible and return quickly to its original shape.

Soles and Linings

The surest marks of a fine quality shoe are leather soles and heels and leather linings within the shoe. It is said that a man exerts as much pressure on the soles of his feet when walking as an elephant. Whether or not this is completely accurate, the pressure per square inch is nevertheless enormous. The sole provides a kind of shock absorber. Good leather does this better than almost any other suitable material. A leather heel provides further cushioning with just enough give to make walking pleasant. Rubber soles give as well but because they will not slide on pavement, friction is built up when you walk. Over a period of time this can make your feet hot and uncomfortable.

Inside the shoe the extra layer of leather that covers the interior seams offers further protection from the cold and gives greater structural support to the shoe. It also increases the shoe's lifespan. Aesthetically a leather inner lining is a handsome detail that separates the fine quality shoe from the mass-market model.

The Waist

The waist is the narrow part of the last where the front and back of the shoes come together under the instep. Like the vamp, a small waist can be helpful in creating the appearance of a more elegant shoe. Instead of having a block look, a small-waisted shoe curves smoothly in and then out, giving a cleaner, more streamlined look.

Vamp Decorations

Loafers with buckles or chains across the vamp have become increasingly popular since the Gucci loafer was first marketed in the United States fifteen years ago. One should be careful, however, not to allow these gold or silver decorations to become so large or gaudy that they destroy the integration of a man's look by drawing immediate attention to his shoes. More effective as vamp decorations are the leather penny saddle or tassels. These work to break up the vamp, thus making it and the shoe look smaller and finer. And yet because they are made of the same-color leather as the shoe, they are not so obvious as to attract undue attention.

4.
ACCESSORIES

MANY MEN feel once they have selected the proper suit and shirt that the accessories can be added with little further consideration. Throw on any old tie and socks, they seem to think, grab the nearest handkerchief. Yet a man's accessories have a great deal to contribute to his overall appearance. They can alter the mood or the entire effect of the attire. Besides, where one must be conservative, even extremely cautious in buying high cost items such as suits and shoes, the relative inexpensiveness of a tie or a handkerchief permits a welcome freedom to the purchaser. The choice of accessories has always been one of the most satisfying ways for a man to express his individuality and unique character. Don't ignore this opportunity.

Ties

A TIE, like a pair of shoes, is a strong indicator of the taste and style consciousness of the wearer. Indeed all your efforts in having purchased a fine suit can be quickly negated by pairing the suit with a bargain-basement tie. A fine, high-quality tie is easily recognizable. It is almost always made of silk, its pattern preferably woven into the fabric, or if not, then finely printed. Other quality ties are made from wool or even cashmere, perhaps the height of elegance.

Ties were originally constructed from a single large square of silk which was folded seven times in order to give the tie a rich fullness. Today quality ties no longer use so much silk. They gain their body by means of an additional inner lining of wool. When you buy a tie, therefore, make sure first you're not paying just for the lining. Feel the silk. Be sure it's soft and has good body of its own. Then check the lining. One sure indication of a quality tie is a fine wool lining in off-white with yellow lines that mark the weight of the lining. If the tie silk is a loosely woven material like grenadine, then the tie is backed by a thin layer of silk so that the lining cannot be seen. Tie linings should never be made of polyester. It just will not hold the tie together well.

All ties are supposed to be cut on the bias, which means across the fabric. This allows them to fall straight after you have tied a knot, without curling. Sometimes, however, the manufacturer tries to save money by not cutting the ties exactly on the bias line. Such ties will never hang properly. Hold a tie you're considering purchasing across your hand. If it begins to twirl in the air it was probably not cut on the bias. Don't buy it.

It is most important to remember in purchasing a tie that its size must relate properly to the shirt collar and jacket lapels one is wearing. In the exaggerated styles of the late 1960's and early 1970's, fat, napkinlike ties corresponded to the wide suit lapels and long-spread collars. Immediately following on the heels of this trend came the narrow-lapeled suit with small-collared shirt and narrow tie to match. These fluctuations are likely to continue on the fashion scene as new designers look for ways to attract attention. My advice is to stick with the classics—lapels and shirt collars in natural proportions appropriate to the individual body with ties that do not approach either extreme of width. This means a tie that at its widest point is no less than 2¾ inches nor more than 3½ inches. Of course if a man is significantly larger than normal, his tie can increase in size somewhat. However what is almost more important to consider than the actual width of the tie is the relationship of its knot to the shirt collar. It should never be so large that it spreads the collar or forces it open.

Unfortunately, though many of the ties now sold are cut in traditional widths, the parts of the ties where the knots are made have remained thick—a holdover from the fat ties of the past decade. Therefore, when you buy a tie, check not only the widest part but the knot area as well. This measurement should be small in proportion to the rest of the tie, perhaps 1–1¼ inches wide.

There are several ways to knot a tie, methods that will result in the standard four-in-hand knot, the Windsor knot or the half-Windsor (see illustrations). With all methods it is important to create a dimple or crease in the center of the tie just underneath the knot. This makes the tie billow and creates a fullness that allows it to drape properly. Though many men consid-

How to tie a four-in-hand knot.

The Windsor knot, because of its size, only looks well worn with a cutaway collar or spread collar with longer points. It is a larger knot than the four-in-hand knot and requires a bigger space to accommodate it. However, in the case of a tie, smallness and precision is the key to elegant dressing.

Four of the more common mistakes men make wearing a tie: A) Too much tie space in the shirt itself. B) Dimple has not been centered. C) Tie has not been pulled up fully into the collar. D) The Windsor knot is too bulbous for the shape and size of the collar.

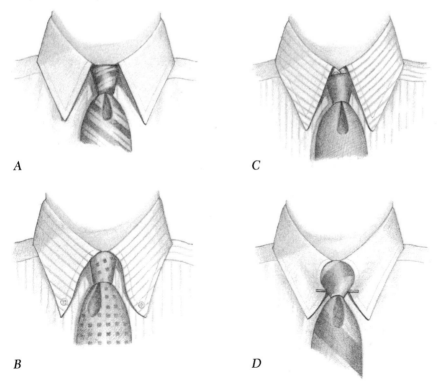

A

C

B

D

ered good dressers (especially in the entertainment field) use the Windsor knot it has always struck me as giving too bulbous an appearance. In any case it only looks well when worn with a cutaway collar, which is how the Duke of Windsor originally wore it. My preference is for the standard four-in-hand knot. It is the smallest of the knots, and most truly sophisticated people agree that the small knot is the most elegant.

Changing your tie is perhaps the easiest means of altering the look of your outfit. A striped silk rep tie or a bright foulard can make a business suit appear less austere, more informal. But put on a small wedding tie, an English Spittlefield or Macclesfield—ties with a bit more sheen—and already you have a dressier, more formal look. A polka dot tie on a dark background will have a similar formalizing effect. The smaller a tie's pattern the dressier its look.

To create a well-rounded wardrobe I would suggest for daytime wear a collection of silk foulard ties, some wool challis ties (which look especially well with sport jackets), striped silk rep ties and several silk grenadine ties, which have an interesting texture for a solid color tie; for evening or dressier day wear, polka dot ties on dark backgrounds, silk paisley ties, several woven silk ties in silver or gray and some small-patterned English Spittlefield or Macclesfield ties. Fine-patterned checks like these are not easy to find, but they are available. They look especially handsome when worn with pin stripe suits, the gray check picking up the gray of the pin stripe.

Bow ties have lately enjoyed a renaissance though I can't say that I've ever joined in their celebration. Worn for formal wear with a pleated-front shirt, they are appropriate and elegant. But during the day when there is only a plain front shirt underneath, that space between the tie and the waist button of the jacket has always struck me as too empty. It appears as if something is missing. Yet if you have a penchant for bows (and some men do look well in this professorial guise), just remember that the bow tie should also be in proper proportion to the rest of your attire. Tiny bows look just as silly and out of place as those huge butterflies which make men look as if their necks have been gift-wrapped.

Yet whether you wear a bow tie regularly or not, any man who wants to consider himself a good dresser should know how to tie one (see illustration). If not for the practical purpose of actually wearing a bow, the exercise will at least give you a better feeling for the correct proportions of tie and shirt collar. You can play with the silk, move it around until it looks just right.

The proper care of your ties begins when you take them off. Never take the tie off your neck by pulling one end through the knot. Rather, untie the knot first, exactly reversing the steps you used when you dressed in the morning. This reversal of steps will untwist the fibers of the tie material and lining and help to alleviate creases.

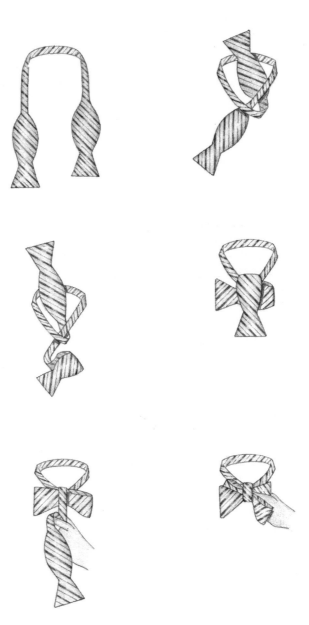

How to tie a proper bow tie.

If the creases are particularly severe, put the two ends of the tie together and roll the tie around your finger like a belt. Slip it off the finger and leave it rolled up overnight. This should return the tie to its original state. Then hang it in the closet. This and occasional dry cleaning is all that should be necessary to keep your ties in fine condition for many years.

Hosiery

A PAIR of hose is meant to keep your feet warm and to prevent irritation from rubbing shoes. That, of course, is the most basic definition of a pair of socks. It can do a lot more. Wear navy socks with a dark blue suit and they serve only their pragmatic purpose. But put on a pair of thin, light yellow wool socks, and all of a sudden you've created aesthetic interest where none previously existed. Instead of a splash of color just at the top of the suit where the tie falls, you now have a subtle response at the bottom.

The best type of hose to buy is that made from natural fibers—cotton, wool or possibly silk. These materials allow a better flow of air, cutting down on perspiration and heat. When they are thin, as they should be (except for sport socks), they are naturally delicate. Indeed, fine socks were never meant to be worn more than several times. They are a luxury, and at today's prices an expensive one. If you can't afford luxuries, therefore, look for sturdier socks, those with nylon reinforced heels and toes.

The length of the socks should be either calf-height or above-calf. Ankle-high socks are definitely to be avoided. Nothing looks worse when a man's legs are crossed than an exposed patch of skin separating the top of his socks and the trouser bottoms. The surest antidote is above-calf socks (which I find uncomfortable) or calf-high socks worn with garters. While garters may sound like a bother, they do keep up your socks and free you from having to wear high socks with their stocking-like effect.

There is a wide variety of hose being marketed today, unfortunately, though, not on the same quality level that once existed. The wonderful clockface French lisle socks of the 1940's and 1950's are nearly extinct as are the real hand-framed wool argyles and patterns from Scotland. (Produced today they would have to sell for more than $25 a pair.) Still with a little enterprise one can find interesting colors and patterns. The easy way out is merely to stick to plain blue or black. But why not try a medium gray wool sock with a dark suit next time, or light yellow or even a subtle pattern? Have some fun. It won't only be your feet that will enjoy the change.

Handkerchiefs

THERE IS a considerable number of authorities on style and fashion who feel that a man is not well dressed unless he is wearing a handkerchief in his suit pocket. I must confess that I place myself in their company. The suit jacket is made with a left breast pocket, not to hold a pack of cigarettes or a pair of glasses, but to hold a handkerchief. Without one, an outside breast pocket appears like an unnecessary design detail. Yet filled with a splash of color it can perk up an otherwise somber outfit or help balance the play of colors between tie, shirt and socks. The handkerchief, like the socks, gives a man one more opportunity to do something a little out of the ordinary, a bit more interesting.

"In the early 1940's," writes O.E. Schoeffler in his fascinating *Encyclopedia of 20th Century Men's Fashions,* "some men were so fond of matching colors and patterns that shirt, tie, pocket handkerchief and even boxer shorts all matched." Obviously no one today advises that kind of coordination. One might match handkerchief and shirt color or handkerchief and socks, but not all three together, and certainly not the same pattern in tie and handkerchief. This custom of matching tie and handkerchief exactly is much too contrived and is the surest sign of an inexperienced dresser. Rather, try to pick up a color in the tie or the socks that might be reflected subtly in the handkerchief. If you're in doubt there is always white. Particularly in the evening a white handkerchief always looks smart for a more formal look.

Fine handkerchiefs were formerly made of linen with hand-rolled edges. These are almost impossible to find today, but cotton serves as an adequate substitute. Cotton fabric absorbs color, lending a softness to the handkerchief that was always the chief appeal of linen.

In wearing a handkerchief understatement is the key. One should be careful, therefore, in wearing a bright silk handkerchief where the colors often have a jarring effect. A safer bet in silk is a traditional English pattern—paisley, foulard or ancient madder. The colors in these are muted and give a more subtle effect.

There are three ways to fold a handkerchief properly—square ended, loose stuffed and three- or four-pointed (see illustrations). The pointed effect, which I prefer, is basically for use with cotton handkerchiefs, especially if the edges have been hand-rolled. Printed silk handkerchiefs look better with the second method. The square end, a popular style in the 1940's and 1950's, seems a little staid today. Yet whatever the method chosen, the placing of the handkerchief should not appear overly studied. The material should stick out above the pocket no more than an inch to an inch and one-half.

There are three ways to properly wear a handkerchief: (left) three- or four-pointed is used with solid handkerchiefs whose edges are hand-rolled; (above) square-ended is very formal and a bit Old World—always in good taste, however, with a solid handkerchief; (below) loose-stuffed is used with patterned handkerchiefs because the pattern is more visible with this method of folding.

*Be careful that the handkerchief
does not become a point of
interest by itself.*

Try using a handkerchief next time you dress. I guarantee it will look better in your pocket than a pack of Marlboros.

Belts and Braces

THE MOST important thing to remember about belts is if you're buying one with initials on the buckle, make certain those initials are your own. Why should you wear a belt with Pierre Cardin's initials or Yves St. Laurent's? Would you wear a ring with their initials engraved upon it?

Personally I don't like belts for dress wear. They cut a man's body in half, interrupting the smooth transition of the suit from shoulders to cuffs. They are particularly disruptive when one is wearing a vested suit. Either the belt creates a bulge under the vest or else it sticks out beneath it, which completely ruins the line.

My own preference is for suspenders. Another alternative is a Daks-style trouser which has small tabs on each side for adjusting the waist of the trousers. No belt is needed.

Suspenders, however, permit the trousers to hang their best—supporting the front of the pants as well as the rear. They are also more comfortable to wear than a belt, which must be drawn tight around the waist to hold up the trousers. With suspenders, trousers can be worn loosely around the body; the only contact you feel is where the suspenders cross the shoulders. When buying trousers to be worn with suspenders, ask the store to sew buttons on the front and rear so that you can use the best type of buttoning suspenders, not the clip-ons. You can also buy your trousers one size larger.

If you decide to purchase a leather belt, make it simple with a small elegant buckle. One of the classics of this variety is made from fine leather cut into three sections which are then connected by two small silver or gold links.

If you want a belt for sport, buy something colorful, a bright red or blue for your khakis or white slacks. You might also consider the old army web belt. A poor cousin of the past, it is now manufactured in a limitless variety of colors. It is functional, long-lasting and will add a gentle touch of humor to your look. For a more traditional feeling there are nice belts of madras and silk rep material, striped or solid.

Of course the most exciting sport belt of the moment is the original cowboy belt with silver or gold buckle. The finest ones are still made in the Southwest out of fine hand-tooled leather. There's hardly a limit on their price. One-thousand-dollar belts are not unheard of though such an expenditure is not really necessary. Twenty to fifty dollars will buy a good one. These belts are classics of a sort and will always be in style. Make certain, however, that the width of the belt is no larger than 1¾ inches. Otherwise it will not fit in the belt loops of your jeans.

Jewelry

JEWELRY IS probably as interesting an investment today as almost any wardrobe item. With inflation likely to continue in the future the price of precious metals and stones is bound to increase accordingly. In terms of actual styling it probably doesn't matter what you buy since the value will depend predominantly upon the worth of the metal and the stone used in fabrication. But if you're concerned about style, the best advice to follow is to keep your jewelry simple.

In general I don't recommend decorative jewelry for men—bracelets, chains and excess rings. But there's no reason why the functional jewelry a man wears—cuff links, collar bars, tie clips, watch fobs and studs shouldn't be handsome and elegant. Leave Florentine gold to the women. Stay away from rococo and baroque designs. Try some occasional humor like a classic Mickey

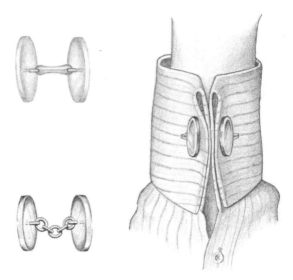

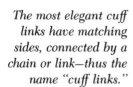

The most elegant cuff links have matching sides, connected by a chain or link—thus the name "cuff links."

Mouse watch, cuff links in the shape of hearts, or a tie clip with a country boot.

Some personal recommendations:

- If you'd like to wear a collar bar, select a gold or silver safety pin style. The clip models never hold securely to the collar points. The proper length of the collar pin is 1⅝–1⅞ inches.
- Don't buy large, gaudy tie clips. A narrow gold bar with a plain design or a small clip looks best. The clip should never dominate the tie or stand out.
- If you wear cuff links, never buy ones with a clip on one side. They look as if you could only afford the gold or jewel on the outside. The best-made cuff links and the most elegant ones are those with matching sides. After all cuff links are supposed to *link* both sides of a French cuff, not clip them together. My favorites are simple metal ovals made of white gold with initials engraved on both sides.

5.
SPORTSWEAR

To THE American clothing industry the manufacture of "sportswear" most often involves the packaging of specific "outfits" and matched "separates" designed to be worn in a given way. This American concept tends to discourage any sense of individuality. I stress American here because this practice is essentially limited to our own country. In Europe men generally resist such programmatic attire for their leisure time. Instead they put together whatever they happen to have around—a sportjacket that might have been worn to work, say, with an open-neck shirt, a sweater with an odd pair of trousers. This requires more thought and imagination than the American approach which would be to don an obviously matched outfit. But the style achieved by the European will be more individual, and in the long run it will be more economic as well. Classic separates of sportswear will not go out of style the way a matched outfit will.

All this is not to say that one should never buy specific sportswear items for use during leisure hours. But one should be aware that the sportswear sector has always been the most fashion-conscious part of the menswear industry. Its designs change quickly from season to season in order to bolster sales. Thus it is the area with the most built-in obsolescence.

The best way to buy sportswear is to be certain that any clothing you select follows the basic lines of the body. Avoid styles that exaggerate particular aspects of a clothing item—excess padding, oversized collars, extra buttons and snaps. Above all remember that your sportswear should represent you, reflect your personality and character.

Americans have always had a strong color sense. Their bodies are large compared to Europeans, and they carry reds, greens, deep yellows and blues without reflecting upon their masculinity. For years men working on Wall Street in prestigious banks and offices have worn somber gray or blue to work. But on the weekends—watch out! Madras jackets, key-lime trousers, bold-colored shirts. Bright colors are fun and they can look great. Use them to express your moods or simply to enjoy yourself. Above all make your casual dressing an individual affair. Certainly in your spare time, in those leisure moments when you no longer have to impress the boss or other associates, you don't want to walk around looking like some European designer or English barrister.

Perhaps one of the building blocks for any leisure wardrobe, at least for those men under fifty years of age, ought to be a pair of jeans. The French designer Yves St. Laurent once remarked that he would have loved to have invented the American jean. His sentiments, I'm sure, speak for most men's designers. The original Levi's jean is a true classic, and an American one at that. Its rugged, no-nonsense good looks, its extreme comfort, its ability to adapt itself to almost any physique, make it an indispensable part of any man's wardrobe.

In recent years fashion designers have been glutting the market with their own interpretations of the American jean. A classic, however, is hard to improve upon. Most of these interpretations are simply expensive, frilled versions of a design whose appeal is based upon its down-to-earth simplicity and utility.

The standard against which all other jeans have had to measure from the beginning has been the Levi's model #501. It remains the paragon today. With its natural, body-hugging cut, its thick 100 percent cotton denim material, its button front and rugged welt seaming, the Levi's 501 has yet to be duplicated. These are the jeans the cowboys wore—durable with a fine, sexy fit. A pair of these jeans could last you two decades.

The only catch in buying a pair of Levi's 501's is that the denim is not sanforized. (These are originals, after all.) They will shrink. So when you buy the 501's, make certain the length is 3 inches greater than your normal trousers. The waist, however, should be an inch larger in size. After several washings, it will shrink and you want to be sure there is a good fit around the crotch and rear.

If you are going out late-night discoing or roller skating, jeans, of course, are perfect. Wear them with a beautiful cotton or silk shirt or with a shetland sweater. If you want something more exciting, black leather trousers cut like the Levi's 501's (a snug fit along the length of the legs) might be more appropriate. These can be worn with silk shirts, T-shirts or whatever else you can think of. Since it is always dark at discos, clothing items that give off light are the most fun to wear—cowboy shirts with bits of cut stone, T-shirts with rhinestones or beading sewn on. Hot stuff, unfortunately, is always changing its face. Remember that when you consider laying out $150 for a jazzy, sparkling shirt that six months later may no longer catch your fancy. Buy such items with extreme care.

For a more classic sport look (weekends in the country or casual get-togethers) wide-wale corduroy trousers, all cotton khakis or a pair of medium weight flannels in gray, heather, green, beige or charcoal always look handsome. Pair these with a crewneck shetland sweater in one of a myriad of colors available, with a well-cut tweed sportjacket or with a cashmere V-neck or cardigan. A fine cashmere sweater made in Scotland now costs over $100, but its cost truly reflects both unrivaled beauty and comfort. It is, in a sense, an investment in luxury. In the next five years the price is liable to double because the supply is nowhere near the demand. Pick colors that enhance your own skin tones. There are no hard and fast rules, but generally, if you're lightskinned, avoid the paler colors.

In the summer, instead of corduroys and flannels, substitute cotton or linen trousers in bright colors. Pale-hued gabardines in bone, pink, maize and beige are as much classics as madras, oxford-stripe seersucker and khakis. All of these have been worn and appreciated since the 1930's. The key here is the cut. Make certain these trousers follow the basic silhouette described earlier (see Chapter 1).

Another summer sportswear classic is the cotton knit shirt by Izod. This shirt, named after the famed French tennis player, René LaCoste, has been without peer in the industry for many years, both for its styling and its quality. It is offered in at least twenty-five different colors and if properly cared for, should last for years.

For a more elegant knit shirt, the nonpareil is made by the John Smedley Company, the manufacturer which formerly produced the English Allen Solly shirt. Smedley produces a fully fashioned Sea Island cotton knit shirt that is the finest available. Its cost is approximately $50. For the cooler months the company manufactures a long-sleeved version in cotton or wool.

If you are on a leaner budget, you might consider the basic American T-shirt at $2.95. Dyed in a bright color, it is durable, simple and stylish.

Sport shoes tend to go in and out of fashion quicker than most fad diets. Yet there are a number which have managed to transcend these trendy pressures. Fine leather cowboy boots have been an American classic since the turn of the century and have recently become part of the fashion scene. They are comfortable, wear well and are great value. But make sure you buy a cowboy boot that really looks like one, not some big-city knock off. This means a boot with a pointed toe and a heel that's canted inward at the rear. Wear them with Levi's or flannels (see picture on page 119 for proper cut of boot).

Other footwear you might consider is the moccasin-style topsider. The leather topsider, first manufactured for use on sailing craft and marketed primarily in New England, is now sold all over the country. It is available in a variety of colors such as emerald green and red. The shoe is soft and comfortable. With its leather upper and bright white rubber sole, the shoe has a great look for all sporting occasions.

The canvas dance shoe, manufactured by Capezio, is also extremely comfortable. Some might consider its thin sole and heel and canvas upper a slightly fey look, but its clean light lines make it extremely elegant. Originally made for dancers, it is now available elsewhere for just plain street folk.

There is a broad range of sportswear being worn today that was originally designed as attire for specific sporting events—sweat pants, jogging shorts, running shoes, hunting jackets and quilted parkas. There is no reason why these shouldn't be adopted for general use. These items were built for function, and yet there is a beauty in the simplicity of their design, in their ease and comfort. When you buy such clothes, it is best to stay away from designer interpretations. Look for the original. Chances are it will give you a greater range of wear. If, for example, you purchased a warm-up suit designed with contrast sateen piping, it might be interesting as a statement about warm-up suits. But if you wanted to wear the trousers with a tweed jacket (a comfortable and stylish look in winter) they would simply be inappropriate except for the most fashion conscious set. Keep your choices simple and functional.

Other areas to pursue for good sportswear are military wear and secondhand clothing. The appeal of military gear is not dissimilar to that of active sporting clothes. The design is basically functional which in most cases means it follows the lines of the body. A military overcoat is heavy and warm and cut long enough to look stylish and keep you in comfort. It is a fraction of the price of a regular overcoat.

Secondhand clothing can also save you money while keeping you in style. For the past ten years people in the know have always included some used clothing in their wardrobes. Clothes of the past tend to be better made than those of today. They are certainly cheaper. And many of the garments have achieved a kind of classic status—1950's pleated flannel trousers, double-breasted evening suits, old cowboy shirts, authentic rayon printed Hawaiian shirts and old tweed coats and vests. These items will no doubt remain in style for thirty more years.

It is clear that the scope of sportswear available in America today is extremely large. Much of it, unfortunately, will not be worth having a year from now. Yet if you avoid the overly trendy and stick with the classics, you will have a wardrobe you can count on—one that is comfortable and easy to wear, that will always be fresh and stylish, and above all will reflect you as an individual.

II. WHERE TO SHOP

6.
THE
UNITED
STATES

Boston

BOSTON HAS more colleges in its environs than any other city in the world. Its better clothing shops are a product of this major enterprise, offering a traditional university look. Don't expect to see much high fashion here—men dress subtly with touches of elegance and occasional eccentricity. Clothing is sturdy and well made, generally sold at prices that reflect its true value. To be sure, there are few cities left about which one can make that statement.

THE ANDOVER SHOP
22 HOLYOKE STREET
CAMBRIDGE, MASS. 02138
617/876–4900
MON.–SAT. 9–6

Tucked away on Holyoke Street in a space not much larger than a cubbyhole, this store has collected a legion of patrons that completely belies its unassuming appearance. The reason for this patronage is Charlie David-son, one of Cambridge's most fascinating personalities and one of the last retailers in the natural-shoulder vein to know the subtleties of English and American custom tailoring.

Charlie, as he is known to everyone, founded the Andover Shop in 1949 in Andover, Massachusetts. Four years later he opened a branch in Cambridge. It is from there that he continues to preside, a diminutive man, rarely without a cigar or a provocative opinion, a friend and advisor to an endless list of critics, writers and musicians who keep in constant touch by mail or phone, sending him their books or records as well as their orders for clothes.

The Andover Shop actually has fairly standard ready-to-wear mer-chandise, a typical selection of Ivy League shirts, trousers and jackets. Where it shines is in its made-to-measure suits, jackets and topcoats, which com-prises 50 percent of its business. It shines here because of Charlie, who has great taste in selecting fabrics and has as much knowledge about making a suit as the masters of Savile Row. But like some top chefs, Charlie needs to be inspired to do his best. If a customer shows real interest, Charlie will respond in kind. He may pull out his special English buttons and linings or some select vesting fabrics he has hidden away. Otherwise he is liable to seem no more knowledgeable or involved than the guy down the block.

The suit Charlie makes is a natural-shoulder model with a shaped body. It is well-constructed and sewn by the Greico Company, with whom Charlie is in constant contact. If you desire, the suit can be finished in the store. An order takes four weeks and suits are $375 and up. Greico ready-to-wear suits are $200–250.

BROOKS BROTHERS

46 NEWBURY STREET
BOSTON, MASS. 02116
617/267-2600
MON.–SAT. 9:30–5:30
SEE NEW YORK

J. PRESS

82 MT. AUBURN STREET
CAMBRIDGE, MASS. 02138
617/547-9886
MON.–SAT. 9:00–5:30
SEE NEW YORK

KEEZER'S

221 CONCORD AVENUE, CORNER OF HURON STREET
CAMBRIDGE, MASS. 02138
617/547-2455
MON.-SAT. 9:30-5

Founded in 1895 by Max Keezer, this is the oldest used clothing store in America. There is nothing hip or fashionable about Keezer's. Its atmosphere is more Salvation Army than *Women's Wear Daily*. And yet for fine secondhand suits, topcoats and tuxedos, there's probably no store anywhere that can compete with it.

For years Keezer's has dressed Harvard students and graduates, including John F. Kennedy who used to buy Chesterfield coats here. In turn these same students supported Keezer, bringing in their suits and coats for ready cash. A particularly opportune moment to make "finds" was always following the Harvard-Yale football game. Lost bets had to be paid and the easiest way to raise cash was at Keezer's. Often some of the wealthy students would have suits made by their fathers' tailors which they brought directly to Keezer, who could always be counted on to cover their drinking bills.

While college students are not so high-spirited in Cambridge as they once were, Keezer's still manages to collect wonderful things. The owner pays cash for used Brooks Brothers, J. Press, Polo, Paul Stuart and custom-made suits, then resells them at reasonable prices. Suits may cost $45-60, topcoats $50, old tuxedos $38.50. On occasion Keezer will have a raccoon coat, which at less than $100 is an absolute bargain.

Don't be upset if you don't find anything to buy during your first visit. Try again the next time the stock market falls. Keezer's is like that.

L. L. BEAN

FREEPORT, MAINE 04033
207/865-3111
24 HOURS A DAY, 7 DAYS A WEEK

The L. L. Bean store, which houses the world's largest collection of outdoorsman's apparel and accessories, is a modernized warehouse of strictly utilitarian design. Its lack of distinction, however, seems almost beside the point. There are 1.5 million L. L. Bean customers nationwide, most of whom will never see the store. They shop by the 100-page Bean catalogue, sent out several times a year and bringing back between 3000 and 30,000 orders a day.

Founded in 1912 by the New England sportsman, Leon Leonwood Bean, the company is run today by Bean's grandson, Leon Gorman. It carries everything from tents and down sleeping bags, to khakis, parkas, Pendleton shirts, shetland sweaters and shoes. In the New England tradition Bean sells value and durability. Its clothing line rarely changes from year to year and remains fairly inexpensive. Mid-wale corduroy trousers, for example, are $23.25; oxford-cloth shirts are $16.00. The style could be roughly characterized as "rugged university."

Perhaps Bean's most famous product is its Maine hunting shoe. Vice President Mondale arrived at Bean's last year with twenty-two Secret Service men in tow just to try one on. Made with rubberized bottoms and leather tops, it was supposedly invented by L. L. Bean himself, who felt all-rubber boots were too clammy and clumsy for all-day walking and heavy leather woodsman's boots too uncomfortable. Today Bean sells over 100,000 pairs annually (from $34.00–59.75) and not only to outdoorsmen. The hunting shoe can be seen on fashion-conscious people in cities throughout the world, most recently in a gamut of colors, though Bean continues to make the original in only brown or tan.

Bean will make good on all defective merchandise, and there is never a problem about returning apparel that doesn't fit or about which you have changed your mind. In an era when driving a car is likely to become a premium activity, shopping by mail may be the best way to save money, so, Bean should be high on anyone's list. You can receive a catalogue merely by dropping Bean a postcard or by telephoning the store directly.

LOUIS
470 BOYLSTON STREET
BOSTON, MASS. 02112
617/965-6100
MON.–SAT. 10–6, WED. UNTIL 8:30

Louis was a pawnbroker who taught his sons how to evaluate clothing for loans. Later when these sons opened their own men's clothing store they decided to name it after their father. The name remains, of course, but the Louis of today, run by the family's third generation, is as far from that original little pawnshop as can possibly be imagined.

The store itself has three full floors of men's merchandise with an elaborate tailoring shop on the fourth floor. The floors are stylishly decorated with Persian rugs and interesting antiques. But what makes Louis truly unusual is its "total collection" concept. Each season owner Murray Pearlstein and his assistants put together a new look for the store, a total look for a man from shoes to hat. They rely on exciting displays which are changed regularly to present these "looks" and to help customers visualize the total outfit.

Pearlstein is extremely knowledgeable of the menswear field. Not only do he and his assistants edit the market extremely well, but he also creates his own fabrics which the Hickey-Freeman company makes into suits for the store. Hickey-Freeman is an excellent traditional men's suit maker, which Pearlstein now has producing elegant European models just for Louis ($495).

Louis takes a position on current styles in each department. Don't expect to find a little of this and that. You'll see only what Pearlstein and staff deem stylish for this season. If you don't understand something, feel free to question any of the salespeople. They are exceedingly helpful and some of the most capable and best informed I've come across.

If you have trouble fitting into standard size suits, or if you'd like something a little different, Louis will take your measurements and have Hickey-Freeman make a suit for you which will be finished in the store. Pick from a large group of beautiful fabrics on the second floor, suitings from Zegna and Hickey-Freeman. The whole process takes about four to five weeks and will cost from $500–750. Otherwise select from the highly fashionable clothing lines on the first floor or from the more traditional designer lines such as Ralph Lauren on the third. Suits there run from $300–500, shirts $35 and up, ties $15–30.

If you're interested in fashionable clothing, you're bound to find something you like at Louis. A visit there is always provocative, if not fully satisfactory.

ROBERT TODD LTD.
141 NEWBERRY STREET
BOSTON, MASS. 02116
617/267–0650
MON.–FRI. 10–6, SAT. 10–5:30

Robert Todd worked for seven years as a buyer for Filene's, the Boston department store, before he opened his own store in the heart of the city's downtown shopping district. Filled with antique fixtures, carpeted and furnished in muted fabrics, this store is everything Filene's is not—a tranquil, unhurried shopping space, where the emphasis is placed on discreet, personalized service.

Robert Todd makes a point of carrying nothing that smacks of the "trendy." But his clothing is not staid. Indeed this store is *the* men's store in Boston for the updated classic look. It is traditional clothing with a flair. Todd edits the Ralph Lauren and Alexander Julian collections extremely well, making certain that the suits and jackets he sells will not be quickly dated but can be worn for years to come. Suits in these lines run from $375–650. Todd also carries a well-chosen selection of traditional sportswear—khaki trousers, shetland sweaters and the fine Polo knit shirts. Men's accessories include suspenders and top quality wool hosiery.

Chicago

CHICAGO SITS in the middle of the country and so avoids the clothing extremes of both coasts. One sees here neither the athletic casualness of California nor the sophisticated stylishness of New York. Clothes tend to reflect the general outlook of the population, which is Midwestern conservative. There are fine shops selling traditional American styles, but don't look for anything too racy. "Fashion" does come to Chicago but most often it is six months to a year behind that in New York or Los Angeles.

Men shopping for basics can do as well in Chicago as in perhaps any other major American city. For the one-of-a-kind items, the sophisticated Chicagoan shops elsewhere—in New York or Europe.

BAILEY'S
25 W. VAN BUREN STREET
CHICAGO, ILL. 60605
312/939-2172
MON.–FRI. 9–6:30, SAT. 9–5:15

Bailey's has been in business fifty-two years, and during that time, according to the owner, everyone from kings to bums has made their way into the store. Seeing it today one immediately thinks of the bums. The store is located on a deteriorated block of Chicago's Loop, with a tacky neon sign outside and paint-chipped tin ceilings within. Yet one can be sure that no bum would pay $300–400 for its special custom riding boot or $50 for a pair of jodhpurs.

Bailey's began as a specialty store selling only riding apparel and accessories in the English tradition. It has changed considerably since then, and now its biggest customer is the camping enthusiast. Canvas tents hang from the ceiling of the store and sleeping bags and knapsacks are haphazardly strewn about.

Yet Bailey's also has a strong "fashion" following. These people come here for the selection of authentic cowboy boots by Acme and Dan Post ($95–175), the 501 Levi's jean and Bailey's outstanding inventory of surplus military uniforms. These stocks change constantly, as lots are bought up from around the world, but there are always special jackets, shirts and overcoats. Recently Bailey's had on sale some great pleated summer shorts from the Ethiopian Army. These were made in the lightest cotton chino and were only $12.

Bailey's never has discount sales, but there are always bargains on hand.

BRITTANY LTD.
642 N. Michigan Avenue
Chicago, Ill. 60611
312/822–0190
Mon.–Fri. 9–6, Sat. 9–5:30

Brittany Ltd. is only twenty years old, but with its brick and redwood exterior and dome-shaped awnings, the store has the appearance of an old English carriage house. This is precisely the look and feel that owner Joseph Richards wanted when he decided to open a store for the traditional customer who wanted something more stylish than a sack suit. "We're not doing anything revolutionary," he says, "just trying to build a better mousetrap."

Brittany's reputation has been built on its attention to fit and service for the Midwest customer interested in natural-shoulder clothing. The alteration department does excellent work, making fine all-wool ready-to-wear suits fit like custom-made. There is rarely an extra charge for even the most major alterations. It represents Southwick Clothes exclusively in Chicago, as well as offering suits and jackets from Ralph Lauren and Norman Hilton. Prices start at $175 for jackets and $275 for suits.

Like Paul Stuart in New York, with whom Brittany is often compared (at least in Chicago), there is an extremely large and well-chosen selection of traditionally styled ties—reps, foulards, paisleys and grenadines—all made from fine silk and wool, and silk-lined ($8.50–25.00). Brittany carries long-staple cotton dress shirts and sportswear from Bert Pulitzer.

Sales take place after Christmas and the week before Father's Day in June.

CAPPER AND CAPPER
1 N. Wabash Avenue
Chicago, Ill. 60602
312/236–3800
Mon.–Sat. 9:30–5:30

Capper and Capper has been a Chicago landmark for at least one hundred years. It was founded by the two Capper brothers in 1840, and few

Chicago luminaries have not done their shopping there, including the Windy City's most famous son of recent years, the late Mayor Richard J. Daley.

The store has just undergone a $400,000 renovation, but it has nevertheless managed to retain its Old World, clubby feeling. Entering through the solid bronze doorways, one immediately reacts to the aura of exclusivity and quiet style, a sense of timelessness and authenticity. Upstairs on the mezzanine is George, who has been shining shoes in that same spot for twenty years. Downstairs is a department carrying the handmade Brigg umbrella from England, at $85 the finest umbrella in the world.

Capper and Capper carries a strange amalgam of merchandise, a number of very commercial lines such as Hathaway shirts and Countess Mara ties, as well as some items of international reputation. These latter include McGeorge Scottish lambswool sweaters ($50), their famous cashmere cardigans ($135), a fine selection of English Viyella sport shirts in both solids and plaids ($45) and some great four-button cotton boxer shorts ($20).

Capper suits and jackets are natural-shoulder models by Hickey-Freeman, Walter Morton and Grief, Inc. ($275–450). The shoes are by Church of England and Bally of Switzerland. A specialty in this department is the Church Royal Opera slipper, in brown or black velvet, with a gold embroidered lion on the toe, $85.

Also of special interest here is the gift section. It carries antique brass lighters, interesting tie bars and collar pins. There are also large country-club-sized shower heads at $40.

This is a store with an excellent selection of merchandise, informed by a strong British-American orientation. The customers tend to be older, but there are items here to interest any young man. Sales are in January and July.

MORRIE MAGES SPORTS
620 N. LaSalle Street
Chicago, Ill. 60610
312/337–6151
Mon., Tue., Thurs., Fri. 9–9; Wed. 11–9; Sat. 9–6;
Sun. 10–5

Morrie Mages calls itself the Number One sports department store in the world. It may very well be—at least in size. Located on Chicago's North Side in a neighborhood that one could hardly call posh, it occupies an eight-story old loft building, each floor of which, including the basement, is crammed with sporting equipment. According to Morrie Mages, the sixty-five-year-old owner, the store employs 120 people and has an inventory worth $4,000,000. The store carries equipment and clothes for weight lifting, hiking, skiing, biking—indeed for almost any sporting endeavor one could imagine except for those involving guns. Mages considers firearms destructive, the antithesis of sporting goods.

Most of the floors of Mages are taken up with actual sporting equipment; hockey sticks and scuba tanks, over 100 brands of tennis racquets, and 6000 pairs of roller skates. But in between there is clothing worth shopping for. Mages carries ski parkas from twenty different manufacturers, $50–200. There is a good selection of hiking boots, $28–95 and perhaps the largest offering of athletic shoes in the world, over two hundred styles available.

Mages Sports is thought of as a discount store in Chicago, but actually most of the prices are fairly standard. One goes there not for bargains but for the variety. You're certain to find something you want.

ULTIMO
114 E. OAK STREET
CHICAGO, ILL. 60611
312/787-0906
MON.–SAT. 9:30–6

Ultimo is one of the nation's best known fashion stores, and the pride of Chicago's successful younger set. It's not inexpensive, throwaway fashion the store carries, but the sophisticated styles of the hot European designers. Entering the shop, one could hardly think otherwise. The walls are draped with heavy silk or painted a deep burgundy color. The floor is covered by a rich cream-colored patterned carpet and there are hanging glass chandeliers.

Founded twelve years ago by Jerry and Joan Weinstein, the store became an immediate success, bringing the emerging European designers' fashions to Chicago, for both men and women. Today they carry the Armani "couture" line, and the suits and jackets of Dimitri, Versace, Pitti, Jhane Barnes, Brioni and Zegna. Suits are $300–500, jackets $175 and up. They have shirts by the American designers Pinky & Dianne, $95–150, and a wide selection of silk shirts by Pancaldi of Italy.

Ultimo prides itself on its service to the customer. Its salesmen are knowledgeable and solicitous; its tailoring department excellent. There are sales in February and at the end of July.

Dallas

DALLAS HAS always been a conservative town, both in its politics and its dress. For years visitors from the East looking for real Western wear were told to go elsewhere—to Houston or Fort Worth. Dallasites, it seems, did not want to be associated with the garish excesses of the Houston oil men or the rodeo cowboys. They were quiet businessmen who wanted to project the image of the Eastern Establishment. Their imitation, however, was a poor one. Instead of dressing with a subtle classicism, they managed merely to be boring.

Some of this is changing now. You do see local residents in cowboy boots and with a touch more color in their wardrobes. But old habits are broken slowly. Aside from a few very special shops there is still little to choose from in the Dallas world of men's haberdashery.

FADED ROSE
2720 Knox Avenue
Dallas, Texas
214/826–7450 or 357–2005
Mon.–Sat. 11–6

There are very few shops in Dallas that would interest a knowledgeable dresser visiting from the East, but this is one. Joyce Baker, the founder and owner, began collecting antique clothing for herself some eleven years ago. Soon after, she realized that many of the new styles being touted by young designers resembled those she had been collecting for herself, at considerably reduced prices. Her response to this discovery was to open Faded Rose in a charming 1930's building shaded by black-and-gray-striped awnings.

Dallas is hardly a "fashion" town and it was not easy going at first. Now, after seven years, Faded Rose has firmly established itself with its own decidedly local clientele, an amalgam of theatre people, fashion customers and those sophisticated Dallasites who have been to the East and seen the light.

Joyce claims that any clothing twenty-five years and older can be considered antique. By this gauge almost all that she carries is antique, not used, beginning with her 1950's rayon shirts in pink and black ($8–15) and going back all the way to the 1920's for some wonderful men's suits. Of special interest are the double-breasted gabardine suits of the 1940's ($30–35), authentic Hawaiian shirts of the early 1950's ($12–25) and a choice selection of all-wool gabardine, embroidered Western shirts at absolutely bargain prices ($7–35).

Obviously, being in the antique clothing business, Faded Rose's stock is constantly changing. Joyce Baker, however, has excellent taste, and you are likely to find something of interest with almost every visit.

OUTFITTERS
428 NORTH PARK CENTER
DALLAS, TEXAS
214/361–6032

1004 PRESTON WOOD TOWN CENTER
DALLAS, TEXAS
214/980–1567
MON.–FRI. 10–9, SAT. 10–6

These two stores offer the best presentation of men's clothes and accessories in Dallas. Run by Doug Pickering, formerly of the Britches chain in Washington, D.C., Outfitters sells a traditional Eastern style sensibility to the well-to-do from Mexico and the wealthy professional of Dallas.

The Outfitters stores have a similar look to those of the Britches chain—a clubby atmosphere with English trappings. The store is decorated with brass fixtures, fine rugs cover the parquet floors, and antique furniture is used for display tables. There is also a beautiful gift bar where small men's accessories are sold—collar stays, jewelry and cologne, wallets, shaving gear and suspenders ($12.50–22.50).

Outfitters' suits are natural-shoulder models with shaped silhouettes, made in fine worsteds and flannels. They sell from $245–385. Their shirts are pima cottons and broadcloths for $31–50. Their ties are all traditional in style and have been carefully selected—silk reps, foulards, grenadines and paisleys, for $27–30. There are sales in January and June.

SHEPLERS
2500 E. CENTENNIAL BOULEVARD
ARLINGTON, TEXAS 76011
817/461–0191
MON.–SAT. 10–9

Founded forty years ago by Harry Shepler, this is now the largest firm in the world selling Western-style clothes and accessories. There is a chain of Sheplers stores in the Midwest, as well as a mail-order catalogue business operating out of Wichita, Kansas.

In Dallas, where it all began, a huge one-story warehouse building offers over one acre of selling space. On hand are 3000 pairs of boots, an endless supply of jeans, cowboy hats in as many styles as one can imagine, as well as a collection of Western-style belts, jackets, ties, vests, guns, handbags and jewelry.

Sheplers keeps a sharp eye on prices (boots begin at $50, fancy embroidered Western shirts at $30), so it is no wonder that many of the West's remaining cowboys do all their shopping here. However Sheplers also sells more of the handmade Lucchese cowboy boots ($260 and up) than any other U. S. outlet.

This is not a store looking for the fashion crowd (though they do shop here too) but for the ordinary customer who simply enjoys Western-style clothes at good value. If you can't find a ready-made boot you like here, it probably doesn't exist. This goes for cowboy hats as well as horse bridles or trailers. Sheplers carries it all. And yet for such a large operation, there is still a sense of personalized service and interest on the part of the salesmen that one has a hard time finding today at considerably smaller and more exclusive shops in the East.

Houston

HOUSTON IS a city of new money, its population growing by almost 85,000 transplants a year. These people are predominantly young and anxious for success. There seem to be no bottoms to their pocketbooks. Houston stores are numerous, as compared to Dallas, and it is not unusual for any of them to pick up new $10,000-a-year customers every week. These are either executives of recently booming industries or wealthy South Americans up for a weekend of shopping.

Such a clientele, consumption-oriented and in most cases with little sense of the tradition and history of fine men's clothes, does not lend itself to the promotion of stylish shops. Such is Houston's problem. Naturally all the major men's designers are represented here and they do sell well. But when one thinks of the Houston man's dress, one thinks less of Ralph Lauren than of L.B.J. Ties are Windsor-knotted, men wear large-collared shirts, flared pants and Western boots. The look is big, overdone and generally slick. There are exceptions, and one can find interesting things to buy here, but it takes some looking.

CUTTER BILL'S
5818 LBJ FREEWAY
DALLAS, TEXAS 75340
214/239-3742

5647 WESTHEIMER
HOUSTON, TEXAS 77056
713/622-5105
MON.–FRI. 10–9; SAT. 10–6

Cutter Bill's is a vast emporium of Western-style clothing, but don't count on seeing any real cowhands here. This is a store that caters exclusively to the "drugstore cowboy." Right outside the store entrance is a life-size gold statue of a rearing horse. Inside there are crystal chandeliers, antique mirrors and plush rugs. Hardly a home on the range.

But there isn't a lot of range left around Houston anyway. The suburbs have taken care of that. Still when many of the residents there want to get dressed up, they remember their antecedents and come to Cutter Bill's for the most flashy, Western-style clothes you can imagine—fancy cowboy boots in special leathers, many in stock or made-to-order ($200–2000); belts with diamond-studded buckles ($1000); hats with exotic feather bands ($50–300).

Though the expensive merchandise is of a very high quality in terms of materials and construction, its ostentatious design would put a severe limit on its wearability for most men outside of Houston.

Still there is always a feeling of excitement in the air at Cutter Bill's. Men and women dressed in their finest Western-style duds crowd the store, their jewelry and silver spurs clinking as they examine the colorful merchandise, and spend huge sums of money or just enjoy themselves over a drink on the house. But you don't have to buy to share the entertainment. Admission is free and Cutter Bill's is worth the visit.

LESLIE & CO.
1749 S. POST OAK ROAD
HOUSTON, TEXAS 77056
713/960-9113
MON.–SAT. 10–6, THURS. UNTIL 9

Leslie & Co. is a small oasis in a desert of sartorial mediocrity. Furnished with Persian rugs and fine antiques, this three-and-a-half-year-old shop offers the Houston man an alternative to the normally pallid haberdashery found in its stores.

Leslie, the proprietor, describes his store as "liberated Brooks Brothers," a perfectly apt description. There is a clubby atmosphere in the store which is mirrored in the preppie East Coast university-style merchandise carried here.

Leslie stocks the Ralph Lauren Polo suit line, Burt Pulitzer sportswear, and Cole-Haan shoes. It also has a very fine selection of classic silk ties, reps, foulards and grenadines. This is Eastern conservatism with a flair, overseen by a man with excellent taste.

Suits run from $250–500, shirts $25–60, ties $15–50, shoes $46–125. There are sales twice a year, in February and July.

NORTON DITTO
2019 S. Post Oak Road
Houston, Texas 77056
713/622-7141
Mon.–Sat. 10-6, Thurs. until 9

This store counts among its clientele Houston's most successful and ambitious businessmen. They come here not only to buy the high quality, conservatively styled clothes, but also to see Ben Ditto. Ditto, who buys all the clothes for Norton Ditto, is also a land developer and real estate speculator who can swap stories and boast of coups on an equal basis with even his most active patrons.

Founded in 1908 by the Ditto family, this store has developed almost symbolic meaning in Houston. If you shop at Ditto's, you've become part of the club, one of the city's successes. Small wonder then that Norton Ditto sells more Oxxford suits, the best quality ready-made suits in America ($550–695), than any other store in the country.

Curiously most of Norton Ditto's suits are made with no rear vent. This is a detail Ben Ditto insists upon from his manufacturers, believing it makes the suit look neater. Such a concern would seem to indicate a real interest in special styling, but unfortunately this seems to be the sole indicator. Like the general style of Houston itself, the clothing at Norton Ditto is expensive but hardly exciting. Even so you might enjoy visiting this gathering spot of the Houston business elite—at least to take a peek at the "club."

Shirts start at $40, ties at $25. There are sales twice a year, in January and August.

STELZIG'S
410 LOUISIANA STREET (AT PRESTON—P.O. Box 727)
HOUSTON, TEXAS 77001
713/223–4344
MON.–FRI. 9–5:30, SAT. 9–5

This downtown store sits amidst the huge skyscrapers that now dot the Houston landscape, almost as a wonderful reminder of the city's past. Founded 110 years ago to service the local cowhands and farmers, Stelzig's still has the look and smell of an authentic Western emporium. Now, however, its clientele has broadened to include most of the local horse set as well as the Houston suburbanites. This shop places no distinctions among its customers, and they often say here, "We do not charge extra for the smell."

The shop is filled with a huge selection of leather dress saddles, harnesses, reins and lariats. This is a major part of the store's business as are the tons of horse shoes, custom-made chaps and pistol holsters they sell each year.

But Stelzig's also has an extensive collection of Western-style clothing in almost all price ranges. In stock, in addition to the standard calfskin boots ($75) are cowboy boots made from eel, pigmy alligator and hornback lizard ($350–750). Hand-tooled leather belts start at $17 and silver belt buckles are $25. There are also embroidered cowboy shirts at $30 and up, Stetson hats and unusual hat bands ($3.95 for those made of feathers, $35.00 for one made from silver coins).

Stelzig's has a storewide sale each June. It also has an impressive catalogue, available by writing to Stelzig's, Preston at Louisiana, P. O. Box 727, Houston, Texas, 77001.

Los Angeles

LOS ANGELES is the second major fashion center in the United States, after New York. Yet life in LA is so much more casual than that on the East Coast, and the clothes often reflect this difference in both color and style. Except for lawyers and bankers you rarely see a businessman wearing a tie. Indeed, the California Supreme Court has recently heard an argument contesting the legality of a restaurant policy that denied admission to a customer not wearing one.

Shopping well in Los Angeles is not always an easy matter. Particularly in Beverly Hills there are vibrations in the air that make a visitor want to buy. It's the swarming activity in the shops perhaps, or just the sense that so much money is being spent. There are, of course, many lovely things for sale, often displayed in the most inviting manner. But for good value, one needs to shop circumspectly. European imports, because of the extra costs of transportation to California, are more expensive here. Other items are simply marked up at a much higher percentage than elsewhere in the country. Fortunes, as it has often been said, are made here overnight and spent the next day. The retailers in Los Angeles seem to take full advantage of this situation.

Shopping in Beverly Hills one is constantly aware of the richness of America and the luxury available here. But one is also aware of the excesses such richness brings.

CARROLL AND CO.
466 N. RODEO DRIVE
BEVERLY HILLS, CALIF. 90210
213/274-7319
TUES.–SAT. 9:30–6, MON. 9:30–9

Thirty years ago in Los Angeles a transplanted Easterner had a tough time buying a button-down collar shirt or a traditional rep tie. One of those dissatisfied transplants decided to do something about it. Dick Carroll, a displaced university man himself, opened his own store. He bought his merchandise to satisfy others like himself—the natural-shouldered Eastern customer who had migrated to the West.

Today Carroll and Company is one of the most popular stores in Los Angeles with customers that include many of Hollywood's TV and film personalities. Because of these people's high visibility, Carroll believes he has made an important contribution to the promulgation of the British-American clothing tradition in America. Rightfully so.

The shop carries everything for the man except a haircut and a shave. Carroll has shirts, slacks, suits, sportjackets, casual and dress shoes, jewelry and luggage. Much of the apparel is carried under the store's private label. It is traditional in orientation but slightly more advanced in style than Brooks Brothers. The suits, which begain at $250, are fine quality and an excellent value. Shirts are $25–50, shoes $50–115.

Each year on the Saturday after New Year's Carroll and Company has one of the most successful sales in the country. The store is closed two days before so that all the merchandise can be marked down. It is now a twenty-five-year-old tradition, and one is likely to find 500–1000 people waiting in the line for the shop's doors to open. All of which goes to show that even in Beverly Hills, people still appreciate a real bargain, and there's no reason you shouldn't too.

GIORGIO'S
273 N. RODEO DRIVE
BEVERLY HILLS, CALIF. 90210
213/278-7312
MON.-SAT. 9:30-6

Giorgio's began in Hollywood in the 1920's as a shop devoted exclusively to women. For years wealthy husbands and suitors accompanied their women there and passed the time playing pool and having drinks at the first bar ever in a clothing store. Then about ten years ago someone got the idea that a huge potential market was being ignored. Not long afterwards, Giorgio's opened its own men's shop.

The shop offers its customers an experience in genuine luxury. The decor is old Hollywood elegance with gold and white carvings outside, plush carpeting and furniture within. The pool table remains, as does the bar. The service is impeccable.

The clothing at Giorgio's, directed at the male equivalent of its female customer, is soft and understated. It attempts to adopt an older European elegance to an American physique. Giorgio's carries a wide selection of Brioni suits and sportjackets (for many years considered the finest tailored in Rome), as well as the Zegna suit line, now the best of the Italian ready-to-wear. Naturally such luxury does not come cheap. The suits range in price from $450-1200, and there are *never* any sales. In stock at all times is the famous Giorgio tuxedo, worn by many of Hollywood's top executives and film stars. Made of wool and mohair with satin peaked lapels by Brioni, it sells for $1200.

HARDWARE
8620 MELROSE AVENUE
S. HOLLYWOOD, CALIF. 90069
213/659-4881
MON.-SAT. 11-7

A number of years ago Tom Gilman and Ronnie Romoff could not find what they liked when they shopped for men's clothes in Los Angeles. They were looking for sophisticated styles, not the typical Hollywood gold chain, open-neck shirt and leisure suit look. Fed up, they finally decided to open their own store. The result is Hardware, a clothing store for the hip and sophisticated man.

Ensconced in a pink stucco building appointed with high-tech and minimalist modern furnishings, this store is a pleasure to shop in. The staff is most friendly and helpful. Merchandise is never presented as the *sine qua non*, but offhandedly, or with a sense of humor. The soft sell is disarming and very Californian.

Clothing is quite expensive here, but it is either very high quality or unique to the store. Hardware carries the Alex Julian shirt line ($50–85) and sportswear from Browns of London and Claude Montana of Paris (shirts $50 and up, sweaters $75–175). It also carries some interesting shoes, including several outrageous pairs of specially made Western boots ($250) and unusual quilted cowboy boots designed for motorcycle riders ($125).

This is a store with style and pizzazz, with a personality all its own. There are discount sales in January and July.

HAROLD'S PLACE
416 N. Bedford Drive
Beverly Hills, Calif. 90210
213/275-6222
Mon.–Sat. 10–6

This antique clothing shop has recently moved to new larger quarters, which, in a way, is a shame. In the original store merchandise and interesting artifacts from the 1940's and 1950's were jammed into every niche so that

Original 1950's rayon gabardine Western shirt with smile pockets and embroidery. A collector's item from Harold's Place, Beverly Hills, $75.

one constantly found surprises while wandering about. Now everything has been spread out and carefully organized. This certainly makes shopping easier, but one misses the former serendipity.

Harold's Place carries the usual range of clothing from the 1940's and 1950's, but its specialty is old cowboy shirts. There are always five to ten of these shirts that would be almost impossible to find elsewhere in the United States: lovely cottons and gabardines from the 1940's with terrific patterns, piping and embroidery, the kind of handwork too expensive to be manufactured today at prices most people can afford. These range from $40–75. Once in a while you can even find an old H Bar C embroidered gabardine, the paragon of cowboy shirts. These will cost close to $80, but their quality and styling are practically impossible to replicate today.

JERRY MAGNIN
323 N. Rodeo Drive
Beverly Hills, Calif. 90210
213/273–5910
Mon.–Sat. 10–6

It was in the 1960's, Jerry Magnin believes, that men in Los Angeles finally began to think of clothes as more than items needing periodic replacement. As the great-grandson of I. Magnin, founder of the famous West Coast retail chain, Jerry knew how to put that belief to work. In 1970 he opened his own store, the first men's fashion shop on Rodeo Drive. In ten years Jerry Magnin has become one of the most influential men's fashion stores in America.

From the start Magnin believed buying clothes should be a climactic experience, that the store should give the customer a reason to buy. He was not interested in staid traditionalism but in the excitement of the "new." He made certain his contemporary chrome and glass shop was always filled with the work of new designers, the best of whom he has consistently supported through the years.

One of those new designers was Ralph Lauren. Magnin was so taken with Lauren's designs that he gave him his own shop within the store. That Polo Shop was to lead to many others elsewhere, but excluding department stores, Magnin's Polo Shop remains the most successful anywhere. There you can find the complete Polo line as well as a number of Lauren's advanced designs that cannot be seen elsewhere.

As a fashion shop, Magnin carries no basics or staples. The stock changes constantly. Yet the selection of fashion is on a high level, imaginatively presented and with service to match.

Shirts are priced from $40–75; trousers $55–125; sweaters $50–125. Suits, designer only, range from $350–600.

Magnin puts a lot of merchandise on sale during the last two weeks of January and of July.

MAXFIELD BLEU
9091 SANTA MONICA BOULEVARD
LOS ANGELES, CALIF. 90069
213/275–7007
MON.–SAT. 11–7

You can tell from the front window display that a lot of creative thinking goes on inside this store. The window, changed regularly by the owner Tommy Perse, is always filled with a selection of clothes and artifacts that in combination is a stimulating, humorous or controversial mixture. It is just this mixture that characterizes the merchandise within.

Perse has wonderful eclectic taste. The store itself combines a 1930's decadence with clean, high-tech detailing. An old Telefunken radio plays constantly, while customers browse through the fine hand-knit English sweaters, the one of a kind shirts, the soft wool or linen trousers. Not much merchandise is ever displayed at one time, but whatever there is has been selected carefully and with fine taste by Perse. Always on hand is a large selection of clothes and accessories in black—Perse's favorite color.

This is a shop for the hip, well-traveled set, the styles always one or two steps ahead of the Beverly Hills scene. Of course every fine store in Los Angeles can boast of famous customers, but Tommy's humor and taste appeal to a special breed—Jack Nicholson, Tina Turner, the Eagles, Linda Ronstadt and Jackson Browne.

The clothes are expensive here, but there is no doubting their quality or taste level. Shirts range from $50–250, pants from $50–175, and sweaters from $65–150. Sales take place in January and at the end of June.

NEIMAN MARCUS
9700 Wilshire Boulevard
Beverly Hills, Calif. 90212
213/550–5900
Mon.–Sat. 10–6

This branch of the Neiman Marcus chain, which opened in 1979, is perhaps the most elegant department store in the country. It is also one of the best places to get an overall picture of the current state of fine men's fashion.

Designed by John Carl Warnecke and Associates, the 150,000-square-foot building is clad entirely in travertine marble, a facade elegant enough to compete with its stylish neighbors on Wilshire Boulevard. Inside, surrounding a four-story-high central well covered by a skylight, is a seemingly endless collection of specialty shops. These are filled with colorful merchandise, and with plants, contemporary paintings, prints and sculpture, as well as handsome furniture and cabinetry. This is a store that has been designed to attract the successful and the sophisticated, and to serve them well. On the second floor there is even a barbershop and men's manicurist.

While Neiman Marcus shows little of its own store brand merchandise for men, it always carries a large selection of designer wear. The collections have been edited well by the store buyers so that what one sees is not everything a designer has created, but just his best work.

In addition to choosing fine suit collections, Neiman's buyers have done an excellent job collecting sportswear and casual wear in the medium to better quality ranges. Shirts start at $25, ties at $20, odd trousers at $45. The suit prices follow those set by designer manufacturers, from $225–600.

Neiman Marcus has sales after Christmas and in June.

NUDIE'S RODEO TAILORS INC.
5015 Lankershim Boulevard
N. Hollywood, Calif. 91601
213/762–3105 or 877–9505
Mon.–Sat. 9–6

For garish, outrageous, wonderful Western wear, there is no place, anywhere, like Nudie's Rodeo Tailors. The reason, of course, is Nudie himself, probably the only man in the world who would spend close to $100,000 for a Cadillac Eldorado convertible inlaid with over 1500 silver dollars and deco-

Rhinestone and hand-inlaid glass cowboy belt from Nudie's, Los Angeles, $150.

rated with hand-tooled leather seats, mounted rifles, chrome pistols and a horn that instead of honking plays a stereo tape recording of a stampede.

Nudie began his career in the 1940's working in a factory making Western-style shirts but soon got the idea to have his own store. With the help of Col. Parker, a close friend who became the first manager of Elvis Presley, he opened in a local garage. Soon afterwards Nudie was making custom outfits for a number of Western bands and singers, including Tex Williams and Tennessee Ernie Ford. From there his reputation spread as a Western-style tailor and designer without peer. Today when you walk through the store the walls are crowded with photographs of the people Nudie has dressed—John Wayne, Lee Marvin, Lyndon Johnson—almost any celebrity you can think of.

About 50 percent of the business Nudie's does today is custom tailoring. Whatever the need—a Western singer's outfit or an exotic costume for a special dance—Nudie's can handle it. Recently Nudie himself designed Robert Redford's clothes for *The Electric Horseman*, complete with rhinestones and blinking lights. On the premises are a leather worker, two bootmakers and a woman who sews custom embroidery.

Custom boots start at $275, but there is also plenty of ready-to-wear merchandise on hand, including some incredible rhinestone boots for $600. There are also rhinestone belts for $195 and rhinestone hat bands for $125.

But don't be intimidated by the wonderful garishness for which Nudie's has become so famous. There is more modest merchandise as well, spread out through the store's three display rooms—hats, belts, boots, shirts, buckles, saddles and riding accessories.

Whatever your taste in clothes, this is a store worth visiting.

PALEEZE
708 N. CURSON STREET
LOS ANGELES, CALIF. 90046
213/653-6359
TUES.–SAT. 1–6, OR BY APPOINTMENT

Opened five years ago by Karl Holm and Michael Alvidrez, Paleeze quickly established itself as the best antique clothing shop in Los Angeles. Its holdings are extensive, including a unique collection of fabulous jewelry for women that has been conveniently organized by color.

The shop has a purposely 1940's feel to it, with black walls, Persian rugs, and appropriate 1940's music wafting throughout. It is a comfortable place in which to browse with no pressure to buy. And if you're lucky you might catch a glimpse of some of the Hollywood stars who pop in here on a regular basis to see what Karl or Michael has dug up lately—people like Robin Williams, Jill Clayburgh, Gilda Radner, or members of the Manhattan Transfer.

Stock is constantly changing here, but whatever is on display has been carefully selected and is generally of fine quality manufacture. Of special interest are the old cowboy boots ($90–120), pleated pants of the 1940's and 1950's ($30), and authentic Hawaiian shirts of the 1950's ($25–55).

Paleeze also has an interesting selection of belts and suspenders ($5 and up).

New York

WITH AMERICA now giving men's fashion direction to Europe and the Far East, New York City has truly become heir to Paris and London as the men's clothing capital of the world. It is from here that most of the major men's styles have emanated in recent years; and it is to New York that people now come to see what's happening in the menswear field.

New York has always been characterized by the openness and diversity of its society. It is these qualities precisely that today characterize its menswear trade. There is no one New York man's style, but rather a collection of styles, each of which has generated a whole slew of specialized stores. These stores are in turn a reflection of the vast differences in sensibility of the 8,000,000 New Yorkers living here, a sensibility developed out of their often foreign pasts, from their travel and sophistication and from their ready appreciation of the new and the eccentric.

Currently there is almost nothing sold in the world in the way of quality menswear that is not available here. The variety of shops and the quality of merchandise is simply unmatchable.

Within the confines of Manhattan, New Yorkers can buy the finest natural-shoulder traditional clothing and furnishings in the country. It was here that it all began, after all, at places such as Brooks Brothers and F. R. Tripler, at J. Press, Paul Stuart and Chipp. Of course there are the designs of the Europeans too: French, Italian and English available at any number of a dozen different specialty shops and department stores. Down in the East Village one can find punk and funk wear, across town in SoHo and on the Upper West Side, some of the finest antique clothing shops in the world. Then there are the stores selling Western wear, much of the merchandise uniquely styled; athletic wear; military gear; and finally, let us not forget, those "classics" of Americana: jeans, overalls and work pants, sold here in more quantity than in any other American city.

Yes, certainly, there are cities elsewhere with shops devoted to selling one or even a few of these styles. But in what other city can one find them all, and at such a high level of taste and quality?

Yet New York's fashion is more than only its shops. It is the people too, and designers from Europe come to New York sometimes just to street watch. New Yorkers like to flaunt their individualism, and the way some do it best is through their clothes. With such a large selection to choose from, there is rarely the compunction to confine oneself to a singular mode. The mixing of styles here, the creative eclecticism, is in striking contrast to what is generally found elsewhere. Yet this seems to be the direction men's fashion is heading in, and New York City is leading the way.

A. PETER PUSHBOTTOM
1157 SECOND AVENUE
NEW YORK, N. Y. 10021
212/759–1336
MON.–SAT. 11–7

Yes, there is an A. Peter Pushbottom. He's a pleasant young man with a knitwear factory who five years ago decided to open a retail outlet. The good fortune for New Yorkers is that he decided to open it here.

Peter sells only his own merchandise which consists of a classic line of sweaters done in a marvelous rainbow of colors. The prices are excellent because he has eliminated the middleman. Yarn is imported from Europe, and the sweaters are knit in his own New York factory. Then they are either wholesaled across the country or delivered to the Second Avenue shop. The fully fashioned crewneck in either 100 percent cotton or shetland wool is $36. The cableknit sweaters start at $40.

ARTHUR GLUCK
37 West 57th Street
New York, N. Y. 10019
212/755-8165
Mon.–Fri. 9–5

Arthur Gluck has been making custom shirts for thirty-five years, and his product is one of the finest in New York. Gluck himself is a transplanted Hungarian who started his shirtmaking career in Paris. When he moved here in 1967 he brought his Old World attitudes with him. His carpeted showroom has been elegantly furnished, and his shirts reflect the same care and craftsmanship that have long been a hallmark of Europe's fine custom trade.

Gluck has available over 500 shirting materials in all grades of cotton and silk. Shirts are $70 in all cotton, and he requires a six-shirt minimum order. Shirts take seven to ten weeks to finish.

As a special service to his own customers, such as Alan King and Harry Belafonte, Gluck provides a cleaning service for custom shirts.

For $4 apiece, each shirt will be hand washed and pressed.

BARNEY'S
Seventh Avenue at 17th Street
New York, N. Y. 10011
212/929-9000
Mon.–Sat. 9–9:30

A number of years ago an African ruler began calling all over the world looking for suits in his size, a ponderous 56 portly. He stopped when he reached Barney's. They told him they had forty-four garments in his size, and the next day he was on his private jet, flying north to New York to buy out the stock.

That African ruler learned late in life what many American men have known since 1925 when Barney Pressman first opened his store. If you have an unusual sized physique, Barney's is the place to go. Today the store carries suits and overcoats from 34 short through 56 portly. In a suit size 40 the store always has on hand models in extra-short, portly extra-short, portly short, portly long and regular, long and extra-long.

But, of course, Barney's is much more than just an outlet for the hard-to-fit man. It is one of the largest men's clothing stores in the world, carrying a diversity of clothing styles that is unparalleled.

Yet don't get the idea that Barney's bigness is overwhelming. The store is segmented into smaller shops, each with its own sales personnel who will service customers with the same consideration given a man shopping in a tiny specialty boutique. There are more than 200 tailors (one out of every four employees), and most alterations are made free of charge.

Out of the seven floors of the building, five are devoted to men's clothes. (The other floors have women's clothes and offices.) On the left side of the floors are the European and high-fashion shops. Barney's pioneered in the United States the clothing of Giorgio Armani, Alexander Julian, Versace, Castelbajac and Thierry Mugler. It continues to sell the work of these fine designers.

On the right side of the floors, Barney's maintains without a doubt the greatest selection of fine traditional suitings in the world, at prices ranging from $200–650. These include suits, jackets and trousers from Daks, Aquascutum, Burberry, Norman Hilton, Hickey-Freeman, Chester Barrie and Oxxford. Both Hickey-Freeman and Oxxford suits can be ordered made-to-measure at 20 percent above their normal prices ($540 for Hickey-Freeman, $690 for Oxxford).

Each Labor Day weekend Barney's has a sale that has become famous in New York. It's called the "Warehouse Sale" because all sale merchandise is sold in the warehouse across the street from the main store. People line up for blocks waiting to get at the choice selections, many selling at half their regular prices.

Yet one doesn't have to wait until Labor Day for good value. Barney's is open the entire year. And if it doesn't have what you're looking for, you'll probably have to have it custom-made.

BLOOMINGDALE'S
59TH STREET & LEXINGTON AVENUE
NEW YORK, N. Y. 10022
212/355–5900
MON.–SAT. 9:45–6, MON. & THURS. UNTIL 9:30

As a department store Bloomingdale's probably has no equal in the world. It carries the newest and best of almost every consumer item, displaying them and promoting them with an excitement and personality that is all its own.

As a men's store it is something else again. Men hear the name Bloomingdale's and they expect to see fashion merchandise. That was the case in the early 1960's when Bloomingdale's had some of the top men's buyers in the field, and they were constantly going out on a limb, taking a positive stance about a certain point-of-view in dressing. But today though Bloomie's

The classic leather topsider updated in bright colors of red, green and yellow by Cole-Haan. There are many versions of this shoe now on the market, but the Cole-Haan is the top-of-the-line. It is made of fine leather and cut with a short vamp, $65.

still carries fashion clothes, this area is just of superficial interest. The real business of Bloomingdale's is men's basics, carried in great quantities and with many options.

The tie holdings, for example, are the largest in New York. All cut in a width of 3–3½ inches, they are fine quality silks, wools and cottons, $15–25. On any given day, 8,000 ties will be displayed on the floor.

The dress shirt department has extraordinary depth. Certainly in New York it has the widest selection of better, all-cotton shirts in the $20–40 range. These shirts are either made especially for Bloomingdale's or carry the name of some of Europe's and America's finest designers. They come in a good range of sizes, 14½–17 neck, and in an endless array of collar styles, stripings and patterns.

If you want a raincoat, Bloomingdale's has no equal. It has the largest Aquascutum and Burberry business in the country.

In addition Bloomingdale's has a large shoe department and a fine traditional suit department, with a special Ralph Lauren boutique. The quality of the materials is always first rate, the styling fairly traditional.

Men's leather accessories are another Bloomingdale's specialty. Look for a big selection of wallets, key cases, passport folders and small travel bags.

There is probably nothing you can't find at Bloomingdale's if you look hard enough. The crowds may daunt you but if you have the strength, persist. You'll love the diversity, and if an item isn't quite right when you get it home, there is never a question about returning merchandise. Bloomingdale's guarantees anything it sells.

BROOKS BROTHERS
346 MADISON AVENUE
NEW YORK, N. Y. 10017
212/682–8800
MON.–SAT. 9:15–6

There is little that has not already been written about Brooks Brothers, the country's founding father of traditional menswear. Begun in 1818, the Brooks mentality is simply the most important contribution America has made to the world of men's fashion.

The strength of Brooks Brothers lies in the fact that it has never wavered from its original conception of what the traditionally minded American male wants to wear. Yet this strength has proved somewhat of a weakness as well.

Brooks Brothers employed its own clothing designer some 60 years ago but since then it hasn't felt the need to use one. Thus its clothes tend to be traditional to the point of actually looking square or dated. Of course many older gentlemen are used to this look and continue to buy the same Brooks merchandise year after year. But for the younger man most of Brooks's clothing is cut so full that it loses a sense of line or style.

Still Brooks has some wonderful merchandise to offer. Its shoes are without a doubt the best ready-to-wear models available in America. Particularly special are its Peale cap toe oxfords ($275) and its suede oxford bucks ($125). Its calfskin slippers ($38) are a joy to wear.

The Brooks 2 7/8-inch striped rep ties ($15) are perfect for the new fashions and are certain to remain in style. Because the store manufactures the ties itself, buying material and making the ties in large quantities, it is able to save the consumer $5–10 on comparable merchandise. Their button-down oxford-cloth shirt with the famous Brooks roll to the collar still represents at $25 the best value and style in town.

Europeans come to Brooks Brothers to buy their pajamas—in fine cotton cloth, and baggy of course. They also enjoy the special gift items, the leather Brooks daily diary and the shoe bags for traveling made of brushed cotton shirtings.

Brooks Brothers is now a national chain of twenty-one stores and there has been somewhat of an erosion in the quality of their merchandise, due no doubt to the store's interest in keeping fine clothes affordable. Yet dollar for dollar, there is still no store anywhere to match Brooks for its conservatively styled, dependably wearable goods.

The cap-toe oxford made by Peale in England only for Brooks Brothers. The finest English, ready-to-wear shoe available. Bench-made in a last that dates from the early 1900's, $275.

The Brooks Brothers oxford suede classic, $125.

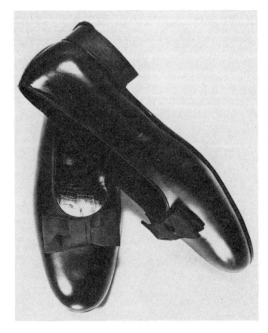

Calf pump from Brooks Brothers—the only calf dress pump available in the U.S. Others in patent leather only, $130.

The Brooks Brothers slipper. So comfortable and available in four shades of leather—brown, black, navy and burgundy, $38.

Two and seven-eighth-inch width ties by Brooks Brothers. A standard for years, it has gained renewed interest with the narrowing of contemporary ties, $15.

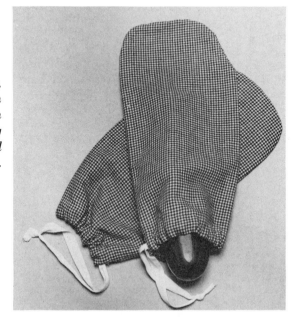

Shoe bags for traveling, made from brushed-cotton shirtings. These are from Brooks Brothers, the only store in America still carrying them, $5.

CAMOUFLAGE
141 EIGHTH AVENUE
NEW YORK, N. Y. 10011
212/741–9118
MON.–FRI. 12–7, SAT. 11–6

The clothing mentality of this shop vacillates somewhere between Saks Fifth Avenue and a basic Army-Navy store, a point-of-view that seems highly appropriate for the hip young man of today. Camouflage carries jeans, painter's pants and Western shirts, as well as $300 suits from some of America's top young designers. The unifying vision here is the belief in American design, whether it be high-styled suitings or classic jeans and work clothes.

Camouflage prides itself on spotlighting new designers. They were the first to show the work of Jhane Barnes. They also helped to launch the clothes of Joe Collins and the shirts of Glen Patrick McGrary. But what has always made this store provocative from the day of its opening in 1976 was the placing alongside these designs such undesigned clothes as the brightly colored football jerseys ($12.50) and the gray cotton Texaco Man pants ($25) that remain some of Camouflage's biggest sellers.

The owners of Camouflage, Gene Chace and Norman Usiak, had an unusual vision of American design which has gained increasing acceptance with each passing day. Rather than impose a total design on customers they

Industrial khaki pants from Camouflage, New York. These trousers improve with age. Wash them in a machine, beat them up—they look even better. At $25, a great buy in pants.

give them an eclectic choice and ask them to style themselves. They believe in functional, classic clothes with a twist, and that is what men are buying. Sales take place in January and July.

CHARIVARI FOR MEN
58 WEST 72ND STREET
NEW YORK, N. Y. 10023
212/787-7272
MON.–FRI. 11–8, THURS. UNTIL 9, SAT. 10–6:30

2339 BROADWAY
NEW YORK, N. Y. 10024
212/873-7242
MON.–FRI. 11–7, THURS. UNTIL 8, SAT. 10–6

Charivari for Men is only one of four Charivari stores bringing high fashion to New York's Upper West Side but it is undoubtedly the store closest to the heart of Jon Weiser, who runs the Charivari group with his mother and sister. The clothes in this store are really Jon's collection, the direct ex-

*All-wool turtleneck sweater,
knitted in Italy for Charivari,
New York, $80.*

pression of his taste and sensibility. Whether it be Giorgio Armani suits or Ralph Lauren shirts, no item comes into this store that does not reflect his own progressive thinking about current men's fashion. It is a point-of-view that has evolved through the years, following the sways of the fashion market. But throughout that time Weiser has never lost sight of his original goal: to bring style *and* quality to the Upper West Side. He continues to do so.

The first Charivari store opened in 1966. The creation of Selma Weiser, Jon's mother, it was purely a women's shop, the first on the West Side catering to other than little old ladies. So quickly did it become successful that Jon decided there must be men's business here as well. Charivari for Men opened in 1971.

The original intention was to make the store a West Side Paul Stuart. But Jon was soon bringing items in from Europe, and the store gradually changed its orientation. Today Charivari represents Cerruti's biggest client in the United States. It is also a major buyer of Missoni apparel. Other designers represented include Thierry Mugler, Marcel Lassance, Jhane Barnes, Giorgio Armani and Ralph Lauren.

The store has a clean modern look with suits, shirts, ties and shoes displayed in their own separate areas. Suits range in price from $275–500. Shoes start at $50, shirts at $35. Charivari also has interesting sweaters and knit shirts. These are designed by Weiser himself, and manufactured for the shop in Italy. A Weiser classic in this field is an oversized wool turtleneck— great for strolling about in on fall afternoons. It sells for $80.

Though custom tailoring is only a small part of the business, Charivari can make custom suits and jackets in a week's time. Suits are $650, sport-jackets $400–450. Charivari constantly has four tailors at work, and they do excellent fitting and alterations.

One must be aware that Charivari is a fashion store bent on carrying the newest creations. What you buy there this year will probably not be sold there next year.

CHIPP
14 East 44th Street
New York, N. Y. 10017
212/687–0850
Mon.–Sat. 9–6

Chipp sells tradition with a sense of humor. And that doesn't mean the salesmen tell jokes. Rather, in contrast to the seriousness of the clothes at such places as J. Press or Brooks Brothers, Chipp offers classic merchandise in

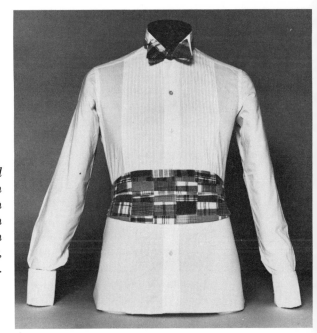

Patch-madras bow tie and matching cummerbund from Chipp in New York. Great fun and thoroughly appropriate in summer, $35. Also available in challis wool paisley for winter, $35.

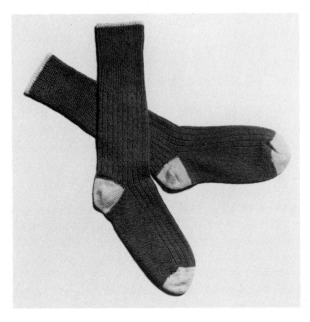

The indestructible boot sock. Made of shetland yarn from Scotland in bright colors with contract toe and heel. Chipp, New York, $13.

slightly offbeat, tongue-in-cheek interpretations. They will sell fine silk rep ties with unusual motifs—a turtle, say, with a tennis racquet. Or they will do a bow tie and cummerbund out of plaid madras. Not long ago they made up a man's athletic supporter in a tartan plaid.

The men who founded Chipp, three former salesmen at J. Press, believe that even corporate executives can have a good time dressing. So in addition to a fine selection of traditional, natural-shoulder suits and coats, they carry some of the brightest cotton pants imaginable, and bow ties in pink and sky blue. In their custom department they will make you a knicker suit out of the finest wool fabrics, $800, or a red field-hunt coat, as traditional as its color is electric, $900.

This is a store with imagination, a place to go if you're looking for something out of the ordinary, but in the classic mold. Men have come here to have seersucker suits and madras sportjackets custom-made just because they fell in love with these inexpensive fabrics and wanted them to fit in a certain way. Citibank came here for matching tie and vest sets for its top executives.

Chipp is that kind of place. If it feels the challenge, there's nothing it won't try to do—especially if it's too offbeat for Brooks Brothers.

DeCASI FASHIONS INC.
37 West 57th Street
New York, N. Y. 10019
212/421-3585
Mon.-Fri. 9-5:45, Sat. 9-1

DeCasi, custom tiemaker, is one of the last of a dying breed. Today it is almost impossible to have ties made to your own specifications, but DeCasi not only continues this Old World practice, but somehow manages to sell its products at competitive prices. Its four-in-hand ties sell for $25–35, prices that one pays for many stock ties in fine ready-to-wear stores. Bow ties are $22.50.

DeCasi was founded by Mrs. Sica, who for many years made ties in the workrooms of Sulka, at one time the finest tiemaker in the world. After her husband was made store manager, she decided to go out on her own. ("Casi") is reversed syllables of "Sica.") Up until the time she retired, she made ties for many of New York's top dressers. Ralph Lauren, who actually began his design career in the tie business, learned his craft from her. Today the store is owned by the tailor, Henry Stewart.

DeCasi ties can be ordered with specifications as to the length, the width, and the size of the knot. Each tie is cut one at a time from pure silk cloth. No mixtures, no polyesters are ever used. The choice of materials, though not enormous, is extensive enough to inspire any buyer. The linings are made from 100 percent fine-grade wool. In addition to ties, DeCasi makes sumptuous cashmere/silk scarves with hand-sewn silk fringes, $75. No minimum order is required, but one should expect a wait of a week to ten days for the making.

DUNHILL TAILORS
65 EAST 57TH STREET
NEW YORK, N. Y. 10022
212/355–0050
MON.–SAT. 9:30–6; JULY & AUG. CLOSED SAT.

This firm, to the surprise of many, has absolutely no connection with the English tobacconist, Alfred Dunhill. Even so its aura of refinement has often been enough to intimidate some of New York's most sophisticated shoppers. This is too bad, really, because though Dunhill tends to be expensive, there are many stores in the city equally so, and without their quality and style. Recognizing this, Dunhill has recently undergone a renovation with the intention of lightening and brightening the atmosphere. The decor of the store has, in my opinion, suffered from these changes, but if it encourages more people to learn about Dunhill, so much the better.

Under the direction of Leon Block, Dunhill has gained a large measure of its reputation both here and abroad from the fine workmanship and design of its custom-made suits. These are now $1000. But equally impressive are their ready-to-wear suits which are less than half that price, $350–500.

Swiss cotton voile briefs, designed by Leon Block for Dunhill, New York, $16.50

These suits are all made from top quality English fabrics. The pieces are cut in the sub-basement of the Dunhill shop, then sewn up in several outside factories. No material is ever fused. The cut is clearly English, with high armholes, smooth chest and tapered waist. For the price, there is probably no better made ready-made suit anywhere in the world.

Dunhill also makes its own fine quality shirts, $35–55, and ties, $20–40. The tie department is especially active. Indeed Dunhill claims to sell more ties per square foot than any other store, 125,000 per year out of a 100-square-foot area.

For the wealthiest of its clientele Dunhill offers fur coats, $3000 and up, and special Swiss voile underwear, $16.50.

Dunhill has it all, from inside to outside.

EARLY HALLOWEEN
180 NINTH AVENUE
NEW YORK, N. Y. 10011
212/691-2933
TUES.-SAT. 1–7

Actor Art Ostrin and his sister Joyce first became interested in antique and vintage clothes in the late 1960's while on tour around the country. Since then, they say, "We have been collecting all the old clothes we could find, just because they are beautiful and deserve another life." Actually many of the things they sell at Early Halloween are just embarking on their first lives. They are products of the 1940's and 1950's which have never been worn.

Early Halloween does a large theatrical business, which makes sense in view of the background of the owners. But it is also an indication of the quality and authenticity of their period merchandise, as well as the amplitude of their stock. On any given day Halloween is liable to have more than 1000 pair of shoes on hand, a good number still new though produced in the 1940's. These include white bucks, oxfords, and some wonderful two-tone wing tips, black-and-white and brown-and-white. Shoes range from $15–45, the higher priced shoes in most cases unworn.

Other items of interest include "new" 1940's hats, $25, cotton socks, $3, and sensational knit suspenders from the 1930's complete with leather fittings, $12.50. There is also a fine stock of 1940's pleated pants, $28–45.

The Ostrins claim that Early Halloween has the largest selection of antique clothes of any shop of its kind. They may very well be right. The place is absolutely crammed with clothes, shoes, accessories and memorabilia. No wonder so many plays and films of recent date have included the credit line, "Clothes from Early Halloween."

E. VOGEL
19 Howard Street
New York, N. Y. 10013
212/925-2460
Mon.–Fri. 8–4:30, Sat. 9–2, summer closed Sat.

This firm makes some of the finest riding boots in the world. It supplies boots for members of the United States Olympic and Equestrian teams, for distinguished tack shops in Europe and Asia and for countless numbers of non-equestrian shoppers who appreciate a fine custom-made leather boot.

The Vogel workshop and salesroom are headquartered in a narrow three-story brick building which dates from 1872—seven years older than the firm itself. It is still a family run operation. Harry Vogel Jr., grandson of the founder, cuts the patterns and the leather while brother Jack makes the lasts to shape the boot. All the boots are made of supple leather, unlike the normally stiff English boots.

Vogel boots start at $178 for the low-cut jodhpur model. The high dress boot is $272. Numerous styles are available, including Field, Newmarket, three-strap and Wellington. And you can order any variation, such as a wraparound with a strap closing, a boot that zips or laces, has sheepskin lining, or which is standardly designed in an unconventional material. Normal delivery time is six to eight weeks. The staff is friendly and helpful, and you will own a boot that not only feels comfortable, but with proper care will last for decades.

Vogel also custom-makes shoes, but they have a heavy look and the designs are not particularly well conceived.

F. R. TRIPLER & CO.
366 Madison Avenue
New York, N. Y. 10017
212/682-1760
Mon.–Fri. 9–5:45, Sat. 9–5:30

Established in 1886 by the Tripler family, Tripler has long been a New York City institution. It sells only the finest quality merchandise available, each item made from select natural fibers. More American in orientation than English, Tripler carries the largest stock of John Smedley shirts, Hickey-Freeman clothing, and sized hosiery in America.

There is nothing modern or trendy about Tripler. Chances are if your great-grandfather once shopped at the store, he would find it little changed today. The atmosphere is that of a fine men's club, with salesmen and customers speaking in discreet tones as they move about the elegant store with its rich wood-paneled walls and parquet floors. When a customer enters the store there is always someone to greet him at the door. It could be one of the five salesmen who have been employed here for over thirty-five years, or even the president of Tripler, who enjoys putting time in at the door. Tripler is that kind of place.

It still carries the traditional alpaca sweater at $75, and a six-ply cashmere pullover for $350. For its older customers, it stocks a wide selection of larger-size merchandise. Pants, for example, are available in sizes 38-42. Shirts come in exact sleeve lengths and may be altered if necessary.

Almost 100 years old, Tripler remains true to its heritage as a fine Old World gentleman's outfitter.

HARRIET LOVE
412 West Broadway
New York, N. Y. 10012
212/966-2280
Tues.–Sat. 12-7

Harriet Love was one of the earliest pioneers of antique clothing in New York City. Her first shop on 13th Street opened in 1965. Today she only operates out of SoHo, still carrying the best quality vintage clothing in the city.

Harriet has always had a great eye and her knowledge of the antique clothing business extends worldwide. Clothes in her peach-colored store are never meant to be worn as nostalgic costumes. They are antique clothes with a contemporary fashion point of view.

Most of the merchandise is for women, but men can occasionally find a great gabardine H Bar C cowboy shirt, the finest from the 1940's, $45–75. There is always a good selection of men's shirts from the 1940's and 1950's, $35–55, and sportjackets as well, $80–120.

Harriet Love's stock, naturally, is always changing. But the guiding taste rarely disappoints. This is a true fashion store based on the riches of the past.

H. HERZFELD INC.
509 MADISON AVENUE
NEW YORK, N. Y. 10021
212/753–6756
MON.–SAT. 9–6:30

H. Herzfeld has occupied the same spot on Madison Avenue for thirty-one years. And although great changes have occurred around it during that time, this family-run firm has managed to retain its distinctly traditional personality, where quality and service continue to be offered in a low-key, almost old-fashioned atmosphere.

Herzfeld sells traditional suits and jackets, but men's furnishings are its true forte. Its shirts are made especially for the shop out of English and Swiss fabrics. The prices are steep, $50–65, but the quality of the stitching and the finish of the shirts are unrivaled in New York. Sleeves are shortened without charge.

Herzfeld is also a place to find quality English ties. The renowned pianist, Vladimir Horowitz, buys his silk bow ties here for $15–20. And there is an excellent selection of four-in-hands as well, including silk Macclesfields from $20–30.

The only jeans worth buying. The original 501 by Levi's with button fly and tapered legs, $16 at most stores.

McGeorge cashmere sweaters, the top of the line in English knitwear, are $150. And if you really feel like treating yourself, you can buy some of the finest men's underwear in the world at Herzfeld. In fine cotton voile, undershorts are $15.

HUDSON'S
105 THIRD AVENUE
NEW YORK, N. Y. 10003
212/473–7320
MON.–SAT. 9–6:30

Hudson's is the largest army-navy store in New York, if not the best known. For jeans, workboots, overalls and surplus army gear, there's no better place to go. No wonder Hudson's can boast of such famous clientele as Diane Keaton, Mariel Hemingway, Elvis Costello, not to mention the thousands of fashionable jet-set Europeans who come here each season, like pilgrims to Mecca, seeking the best and the most authentic in Americana, the classics of the non-upper crust.

Hudson's has been at the same address since 1916 when it first opened its doors as a general haberdashery store. In 1940 it began to concentrate on work clothes, and soon the suits and trousers were completely gone, overwhelmed by the uniforms, jeans and workboots that found a growing clientele. Today Hudson's has six mammoth rooms, stocked to the ceiling with merchandise: row after row of jackets, army fatigues, down parkas and vests. There appears to be some basic form of organization, though that is not always apparent. But one can always ask a salesman, most of whom seem to know their stock to an uncanny degree.

Hudson's has the best selection of workboots in New York, and stocks the Sorel, Canadian sub-zero-temperature boot at $44.95. Its range of hiking boots is equally extensive. These boots are priced from $55–110.

The store's largest seller is the Levi's 501. This is one of the few places on the East Coast where you can find a full size range of this wonderful jean, the original unsanforized Levi's with button fly. There is also a good selection of Smith's overalls at $16, and Sweet-Orr overalls, workshirts and pants.

Merchandise changes from month to month, depending on what the owners are able to pick up. But there are always plenty of American army field jackets, $44.95, and those classic black leather flight jackets, $135. What else you might find is anybody's guess, but looking is part of the adventure of shopping here.

JEZEBEL
265 COLUMBUS AVENUE
NEW YORK, N. Y. 10023
212/787-5486
MON.–SAT. 12-7

Alberta Wright, Jezebel's discriminating owner, began her career retailing imported designer clothes from France. Then one summer she visited Portobello Road in London and "fell in love" with the wonderful used clothing markets, their merchandise so marvelously styled yet so inexpensive. Not long after the uptown's first antique clothing emporium opened its doors. Jezebel was an immediate success. In the 7 years of its existence it has gained an international following. It has been praised in publications from as far away as Japan, and *The New York Times* has given the store five separate write-ups, the last a feature on the front page of the business section!

Despite all this outside attention, Jezebel retains a kind of homey quality. If Alberta is not out front to help the customers, you can always find her in the back, ironing some glorious 1940's satin dress she has just gotten hold of, or making a sewing repair on a silk shawl. Entering the store is like visiting a grandmother's attic, clothes and fringe-shaded lamps hanging from the ceiling, old rugs strewn about. You can browse for hours, and no one will disturb you. Or you can ask for help knowing that none of the salespeople will pressure you into buying.

Jezebel's clothes are primarily for women, but there is always a small select group of things for men. Look for rayon gabardine shirts, $15, or pleated pants in 100 percent cotton khaki, $15, or wool gabardine, $25. There is also a fine selection of men's jackets, $45–55. If you don't find something you like on your first visit, come back. Or if you prefer tell Alberta exactly what you're looking for. Chances are, with her sources and taste, she'll find it sooner or later. When she does you can be sure it will be a quality garment at a reasonable price. And it will look in style with whatever is being represented as today's fashions.

J. PRESS, INC.
16 EAST 44TH STREET
NEW YORK, N.Y. 10017
212/687-7642
MON.–FRI. 9:15-9:45, SAT. 9-5:30

Founded in 1909 by Jacoby Press, J. Press is three generations old and calls itself "the last of the Mohicans"—the purist descendant of an original

American tradition. The clothes are collegiate in the sense that they are cut for athletic men who like to move in their suits. Not surprisingly their logo is the fence seen around Yale University.

Irving Press, son of the founder and today the store's guiding light, says he likes clothes that you can wear to bed, then get up in, and still be able to wear to a party. Comfort and ease is the principle here.

J. Press suits are natural-shoulder, cut slightly full in the chest but shaped at the waist. All wool worsteds begin at $275. They look well with their own J. Press button-down-collar shirts, $25–30, and regimental striped ties, $13.50, though J. Press also carries less straight collegiate furnishings, such as semi-spread-collar shirts, $26.50, and hand-blocked English silk ties, $14.50–18.50.

But Press rarely strays far from the image it has built as the outfitter of the grown-up university man. It doesn't need to. Most of its customers begin shopping there during college days and continue through the rest of their years. It counts on the fine quality of the merchandise—corduroy and bright, all-cotton sport trousers, "shaggy dog" shetland sweaters, harness leather belts. And it places its confidence in the rightness of J. Press's classic unchanging style.

JUDI BUIE BOOTSHOP, TEXAS at SERENDIPITY 3

225 EAST 60TH STREET
NEW YORK, N. Y. 10022
212/888-0341
MON.–FRI. 11–7, SAT. 11–6

A number of years ago Judi Buie returned from Texas wearing a pair of cowboy boots that were a gift from her parents. An admiring friend asked Judi if she could get her a pair as well. Then another friend made the same request. And then a third. Judi realized she was on to something hot, and she decided to go into business. She rented a part of the upper floor of Serendipity, brought in some boots from Texas, and began to sell. The stock went quickly. Andy Warhol bought boots, and so did Dustin Hoffman. Then Margaux Hemingway and Liza Minnelli. The craze was on.

That was in 1977, and many other Western boot outlets have opened in New York since then. Judi, though, remains the favorite of much of the fashion crowd. They appreciate her wild designs and exotic colors. Where else could one expect to find a boot in leather dyed purple, gold and green? Only at Texas at Serendipity.

*Custom-made cowboy boots
from Judi Buie in New York.
This model was designed for
the author with his own
motif on the back, his initials
on the front. An investment
in longevity, $500.*

Judi has her own designed boots made up by Justin and Tony Lama, two fine manufacturers, $175–250. You can also custom-order boots of your own design from the Dixon Boot company. This takes six to eight weeks and will cost about $450–600.

Of special interest is the selection of antique boots from the 1940's, $375. These have never been worn, and if you can find a pair to fit, you have a real collector's item. The design, the coloring and the cut are unique. They are simply no longer available today.

KAUFMAN'S
139-41 East 24th Street
New York, N. Y. 10010
212/684–6060
Mon.–Sat. 9:30–6

This firm has been in business 105 years and it is still operating under the same premises. As one Kaufman brother used to say, "Our job is to sell everything made for horse and rider." That they continue to do. What has changed during that time besides the street (all the horse barns have been converted into garages) is the clientele. No longer are Kaufman's customers limited to jockeys, hunters and sport riders. Indeed less than a third of those who shop Kaufman's know the difference between a cinch and a halter. But it hardly seems to matter these days. Men and women both come here for the wonderful riding and Western apparel that looks so well when worn on the street, or at home as just plain leisure wear.

Kaufman's has a unique collection of hand-painted Western boots starting at $250. Standard cowboy boots start at $80, or if you want something really special, there are custom-made boots available at $500. These are made to your own specifications by a shop in El Paso, Texas, and take six to eight weeks for delivery.

The Beatles once bought tweed hacking jackets at Kaufman's. What is more unusual today, but found at Kaufman's, are the long red wool flannel hunting coats, for $600. These are part of the standard dress on an official "hunt" in England. On the street they hardly look standard. Kaufman's will also custom-make English riding apparel. Jodhpurs are $145, all wool britches $135.

Visiting Kaufman's is like taking a step back into old New York. The shop, with its cement floors and molded tin ceilings, functions almost as a museum, with its enormous horse heads and old accessories decorating the walls. And best of all, there is no charge for admission.

MILLER'S
123 East 24th Street
New York, N. Y. 10010
212/673–1400
Mon.–Sat. 9–5:45, July & Aug. Sat. 9–4:30

In the 1930's when Miller's was already almost fifty years old, an auction barn functioned across the way from the shop. Men would go there and buy their horses, then cross the street to Miller's to outfit them. The auction barn is gone but Miller still outfits most of the horses kept privately in New York, as well as many of the thoroughbreds across the country. The owners of these horses buy Miller equipment through the L. L. Bean catalogue and from specially approved stores that carry the Miller merchandise. Miller also outfits the United States Equestrian team.

Naturally if you're not really into horses, all this must seem a little beside the point. Yet what Miller's has to offer is a kind of expertise hard to find these days, especially in Western wear, which is one of the hottest areas in contemporary fashion. Such expertise is the reason that on a Saturday afternoon one is liable to find an equal mix of equestrians and fashion people wandering through the barn-like store, examining boots, hacking jackets and accessories amidst the rich odor of new leather.

Recommended highly is their collection of Tony Lama, Nacona, Justin and Dan Post Western boots. These are real Texas boots, like the kind the cowboys wear with a good sharp toe and a canted heel. And because the salesmen are so knowledgeable, you can feel confident spending $200 knowing the boot will fit just right.

Miller's also has English riding apparel—boots, $60–175, tweed hacking jackets, $80–100, and wool jodhpurs, $40 and up.

Miller's has sales throughout the year on overstocked goods. These can be real bargains—such as hacking jackets that are sold for as little as $40.

MORTY SILLS
7 East 48th Street
New York, N. Y. 10017
212/355-2360
Mon.–Sat. 10–6, July and August closed Sat.

Morty Sills' shop is one of New York's special places. Advertised only by word-of-mouth, this second-floor store often seems more like an intellectual salon than a custom-tailoring shop. Many of Sills' customers are writers and artists. They come here not only for the fine, natural-shoulder clothing but for the conversation as well. There are few subjects Morty is not conversant in and he is a wonderful listener and friend. His cluttered shop is filled with the books and artworks of his clients, many of whom rely completely on his judgments.

Sills started his firm in Cambridge forty-two years ago. When he found that many of his clients had deserted Harvard College for New York he decided to follow them. In the thirty years he has been here his clothing vision has not wavered. "The suit we made in 1953 is the same as we are making now," he says.

That suit tries to reflect what Fred Astaire showed in his clothes. The style is natural-shoulder softness with a little delineation of the body line. Sills' suits are made from individual patterns and require two fittings. Two-piece all worsteds start at $750 and take two months to complete.

PARAGON SPORTS
867 Broadway
New York, N. Y. 10003
212/255-8036
Mon.–Fri. 9:30–6:30, Thurs. until 7:30, Sat. 9–6

Paragon was founded in 1908 and is now being run by the third generation of the Blank family. It is the largest independent sports store in the

All-cotton athletic pants ($7.95) and all-cotton tee shirt ($2.79) available in yellow, red, navy, green, and gray. The basics for any athletic wardrobe.

East, and the place Europeans flock to in their search for authentic American active wear. Two full floors of its loft building are devoted to showing merchandise, much of it discounted to prices unreachable in most other parts of the country. The other six floors are used to store inventory.

Naturally Paragon has a fantastic supply of sporting goods—tennis racquets, golf clubs, football uniforms and baseball bats. But it also has an extensive selection of apparel. The store stocks over 150 models of running shoes, from $17.95–70.00. Warm-up suits come in an equally large choice, 150 styles ranging in price from $18.95–150.00. These come in a marvelous assortment of colors, from canary yellow to aubergine.

On the first floor are T-shirts of every variety, two-tone baseball shirts and warm-up jackets, hockey, basketball and football jerseys. Upstairs in the backpacking department are displayed Woolrich pants, shirts and jackets, down parkas and vests and functionally styled foul-weather gear. There are also hiking boots of all qualities and styles.

Paragon is always mobbed, particularly during special sale days. But the salesmen are helpful, and when you find one he will stick with you until all your questions are answered.

PAUL STUART

45TH STREET & MADISON AVENUE
NEW YORK, N. Y. 10017
212/682–0320
MON.–SAT. 9–6

If I had to let one man loose in New York City to be dressed by a particular store, I would send that man to Paul Stuart. Stuart sells high quality clothing in the classic American natural-shoulder tradition, but it does this with great imagination and with as much interest in the present as it has in the past.

The founder of the store, Ralph Ostrove, believed Stuart must "stand for something," that it must create an image and "stick with it." Begun forty years ago, the Paul Stuart business has stayed within the bounds of the image Ostrove created, based on his belief that quality can always find a market. Today though Stuart has refused to expand into more than one store, it has loyal customers throughout the United States and Europe, with 68,000 charge accounts on record. They come for natural-shoulder fashion that is contemporary and presented in light, elegant surroundings by knowledgeable salespeople who appreciate what they are selling.

Stuart sells everything for a man's wardrobe, including suits, coats, shirts, ties, underwear and shoes. All-wool suits begin at $225, although most are more. These are either two- or three-button models, made in materials that are exclusive to the store.

Shirts come in almost all collar styles: round, straight, button-down and spread, the diversity of their materials matched only by the variety of Stuart ties. Shirts are $25–55; ties, $15 and up.

Shoes are perhaps the weakest aspect of the Stuart panoply, but this deficiency is more than made up for by the tasteful sportswear and the jewelry department, which carries some of the smartest men's dress accessories in New York. Particularly handsome is the Swiss-made all-jeweled-movement Paul Stuart watch.

The Paul Stuart watch. Replica of World War I French military watch—made in France with Swiss 17-jewel movement, $175.

Paul Stuart is for the man who wants the dependability of Brooks Brothers with a little more flair. One can count on what is sold here; it is quality and style of a high order.

PEC & COMPANY
45–47 WEST 57TH STREET
NEW YORK, N. Y. 10019
212/755–0758
MON.–FRI. 9–5

It is hard to believe, visiting Pec & Co. for the first time, that this is one of New York's most elegant shirtmakers. Located in regular office space on an upper floor in a nondescript commercial building, the showroom's decor is spartan to say the least. A metal table, a couple of plain chairs, worn carpet on the floor and that's it. Hardly the kind of shop one would expect to attract the likes of Yul Brynner, Cary Grant, Onassis, and most of the Rockefeller clan.

And yet for years Pec & Co. has been making custom shirts for a good share of New York's elite. They come here knowing they will receive a product fitted precisely to their own physique and put together with meticulous care and styling. Each Pec shirt is sewn with single needle stitching at a rate of thirty stitches per inch. Buttonholes are sewn by hand and real mother-of-pearl buttons used.

The cost is considerable, $90 per shirt with a six-shirt minimum order required. You must have patience as well. Two to three months are needed to complete an order with a sample shirt after four weeks. Cloth is chosen from an elegant selection of bolts on hand or from swatches of readily available material.

ROSA CUSTOM DESIGNS
37 WEST 57TH STREET
NEW YORK, N. Y. 10019
212/751–1485
MON.–FRI. 9–5, SAT. 9–2

If you have several-years-old ties that now seem more like bibs to you, there is no need to throw them away or let them languish in the closet. Bring them to Rosa Custom Designs. For $6 Rosa herself will cut them down to the more fashionable, narrower sizes. If necessary a new wool lining can be sewn in or the ties can even be shortened if they've been hanging too far below your belt. Afterwards they will be refolded and pressed.

Rosa Custom Designs also makes custom four-in-hands, bow ties, ascots and scarves. These are all made by hand and range in price from $20–30. A three-tie minimum order is required. Ties can be made in a day, but the normal delivery time is a week to two weeks.

SAKS FIFTH AVENUE
FIFTH AVENUE AT 49TH STREET
NEW YORK, N. Y. 10022
212/753–4000
MON.–WED., FRI. AND SAT. 10–6, THURS. 10–8:30

Saks Fifth Avenue is an American clothing institution, known throughout the country for the high quality of its merchandise and the service of its dedicated sales personnel. Founded on Fifth Avenue in 1924 by a merger of the Saks and Gimbel families, it now maintains more than thirty branch stores, from Los Angeles to New York.

In recent years the company has attempted to lead the field in the marketing of the better quality men's designers. Indeed, its Ralph Lauren Shop in the Fifth Avenue flagship store is surely the best Lauren presentation to be found in any department store. But Saks' specialness really lies elsewhere than with the new designers. The store gained its reputation by stocking its own select brand of goods, and it is these items, which it still carries, that make shopping here a unique experience.

For example, an old standard at Saks is a lush beaver-collar coat, now $850. Or for those special evening escapades, a black evening cape with velvet collar. At $600, it comes with either a white or scarlet silk lining. Naturally, Saks always has on hand a fine selection of tuxedos; many stores do. But where else today can a man walk in and pick up a set of tails?

Since the early 1930's Saks has been making its own suits, trousers, jackets and overcoats. These are comparable to Hickey-Freeman models in quality, hand-cut but sewn by machine. The suits come in both a "full" cut as well as a slightly trimmer cut. They have a modest suppression of the waist and are slightly padded in the shoulders. Specialties of the tailored clothing line are two-piece silk suits at $695 and cashmere sportjackets, $475–700.

Evidence of the store's continuing "carriage trade" can be found in the merchandise of the smaller departments—hosiery, for one. This department still stocks French cotton lisle socks with clock designs. Anklets are $8.50 a pair; over-the-calfs, $12.00. And don't miss the sized cashmere hose, $9.00 for anklets; $14.00 for over-the-calfs.

Its pajamas are equally tasteful. Incredibly soft Swiss voile pajamas are $100—a wonderful gift item. In Sea Island cotton with piping, the pajamas are $60. In silk with piping, they are $100.

Saks is a wonderful place to visit. If one had the money, it would probably be a nice place to live as well.

SAN FRANCISCO
975 LEXINGTON AVENUE
NEW YORK, N. Y. 10021
212/472-8740
MON.–FRI. 10–7, SAT. 11–6

No store in New York City has a higher level of taste and style in men's clothing than that of San Francisco. Owner Howard Partman tailors every item of merchandise to his own demanding specifications, blending Old World sophistication with modern functionality and *joie de vivre*. The garments one buys here are investment clothes. Wear them one year, put them away for a year or two, then bring them out again with complete confidence. Updated classics, they are as fresh in style as the first day they were bought.

Founded in 1968, San Francisco has occupied its present location for the past seven years. The store has a quiet elegant quality, with polished wood floors, Persian rugs, English leather armchairs and handsome antique walnut and glass display cabinets. Men's and women's clothing is presented in small groupings with Partman's newest designs hung on interesting mannequins and busts from the 1920's.

San Francisco was the first store to introduce men's shirts with small collars as well as men's shirts with wing collars. But basically the garments sold here are less trendy, more classic American of the finest quality and detailing.

Regular stand-bys are the plain-fronted 100 percent cotton khaki trousers for $50, or the same models in linen for $60. Also available on a regular basis is Partman's take-off on the old army web belts. Made with beautiful leather fittings and available in numerous and changing colors, they are only $12. The all-cotton wing-collar shirts are $75. Fair Isle sweaters hand-knitted in wispy fall shades are $125.

But San Francisco has some completely unique items as well. These include a silk crepe bow tie at $25, and a four-pocket hunting vest with pigskin front for $125. This vest has striped linings and a long knit back for extra warmth.

Partman's partner, Michael Fitzsimmons, is a collector of beautiful antique watches. A number of these are on sale in the front of the store,

Pigskin sport vest with knitted wool back and striped linings from San Francisco, New York City, $135.

beginning at $285. Also ask to see the watches made up especially for the store. Like San Francisco clothes, they offer functionality with classic style.

San Francisco has sales in January and July, but don't expect any great discounts. Clothes of the quality Partman sells are bargains at any price.

SEA ISLAND CLOTHIERS
1295 Third Avenue
New York, N. Y. 10021
212/879-9565
Mon.–Fri. 11–9, Sat. 11–6, Sun. 1–5

This shop is named after the famed Sea Island, Georgia, cotton out of which some of the world's finest shirts are made. It offers a clear indication of the attitude owners Kevin and Julie McLaughlin take toward the merchandise they offer in their shop. McLaughlin feels that clothing should not be intimidating. Rather a man seeing a pair of trousers and a sweater should react as if he already knew them, as if these clothes were old friends or relatives. The shop has that same easy feeling—dark wood paneling and deep green walls; women's clothes on the left of the shop, men's on the right.

Because of the small size of their store, the McLaughlins choose to show only a relatively few items. These are carefully chosen, however, and made up specially for the shop in a broad range of colors. An example is their fine combed cotton corduroy trousers at $55 which are available in at least a dozen delicious hues. Another unique item is their silk moire suspenders for $20. Sea Island also imports fine clothes from Europe. A shop standard is their gabardine trouser by Zegna of Italy, $80.

Whatever you buy here, you can buy with confidence. The quality is top of the line, the styling timeless.

SEEWALDT & BAUMAN
565 FIFTH AVENUE (11TH FLOOR)
NEW YORK, N. Y. 10022
212/682–3958
MON.–FRI. 8:30–5:30

This firm is one of New York's fine custom shirtmakers. Founded in 1921, it sets its prices obviously within an historical perspective. All-cotton shirts start at $50, while most orders average $60. These prices roughly rival many of the expensive ready-to-wear shirts sold today in high quality stores. And yet being custom-made, an excellent fit is assured, as well as detailing that meets one's own specifications.

Seewaldt & Bauman has a good selection of materials, all of them preshrunk previous to cutting. A six-shirt minimum order is required.

SHEP MILLER
MAIN STREET & JOBS LANE
SOUTHAMPTON, LONG ISLAND 11968
516/283–2386
MON.–SAT. 9:30–5:30

The Shep Miller store is the special vision of Shep Miller. Founded thirty years ago, the shop is an authentic example of the Southampton/Palm Beach look. The store has eight large windows wrapping around the main corner of Southampton Village, affording an exhibition of color that could rival a gallery room in the Museum of Modern Art. Inside amidst the tweeds and shetlands are high pillars covered in tartan plaid, several old fire engine wagon wheels, a painted carousel horse and on the walls a lovely collection of framed Spy prints.

Shep Miller began his career as a salesman traveling to universities collecting student orders for his Ivy League-styled merchandise. In the 1940's he became the personal haberdasher to many of America's oldest families, making their polo, hunting and estate clothes. The shop that he eventually opened managed to capture both these experiences. For the university grads there are unusual Scottish shetland cable crewneck sweaters. What makes them particularly Shep Miller is their availability in colors such as turquoise, raspberry and peach (at $57.50). There are also trousers in wide-wale corduroy, in flannel and linen. Miller specials are monogrammed velvet slippers, $135, and cashmere sportjackets in a grand assortment of ice cream colors, $450.

There are also Miller's shirts. These are made up especially for the store, of cotton voile and silk from Italy and Switzerland, starting at $75. And they too come in a rich bouquet of colors.

Indeed there is nothing subtle about the Miller styling, but it is not only rich Americans who assured his success. Europeans too have learned to appreciate his characteristically American flamboyance of color. Arriving in New York, many have been known to drive directly out to Southampton just to pick up several of his shetland sweaters in colors unavailable elsewhere.

STEVE
172 SPRING STREET
NEW YORK, N. Y. 10012
212/925–0585
TUES.–FRI. 12–7, SAT. 12–6, SUN. 1–5

Steve Burger left Bloomingdale's employ a few years ago. Bloomie's loss has become New York City's gain. In the four years since its opening, Steve has established itself as one of the more distinguished purveyors of men's fashion clothing in the city. Though the store serves primarily the SoHo community, it has managed to attract customers from throughout the metropolitan area.

Burger, who does all the store's buying, has a fine appreciation for the look of "today." He says he buys for the store with himself in mind as the customer. And what he likes is "style," not fashion.

Thus the clothes one is likely to find on a given day (the stock is constantly changing) will be contemporary in feel, but not freakish or eccentric. Burger imports much of his clothing from abroad, but he also supports young local designers. He carries no suits, but there are upbeat tweed sportjackets, $225, and double-breasted velvet blazers, $250. There is also a small but fine selection of shoes—leather loafers, $60–95, suede oxfords, $65–90 and some interesting French athletic shoes, $60.

The price range at Steve is extensive, since Burger feels everyone, at whatever income level, ought to be able to come into the store and buy something. The salesmen do not work on commission, so one can browse easily in the low-key, relaxed atmosphere of the store.

Sales occur twice a year, the last two weeks in January, and for several weeks following the second week in July.

STEWART ROSS
754 MADISON AVENUE
NEW YORK, N. Y. 10021
212/744-3870
MON.–SAT. 11–6

105 WEST 72ND STREET
NEW YORK, N. Y. 10023
212/362-9620
MON.–SAT. 11–6

Stewart Ross has been selling his own quiet brand of fashion since 1970 when he opened his first shop on the West Side. Called Stone Free, that small store masqueraded as a kind of jeans shop, but a jeans shop with a difference. With his jeans, Stewart sold old Fair Isle sweaters from England, antique reindeer sweaters from the 1950's and baggy corduroys. Stone Free continues today, even after Stewart moved to Madison Avenue with his second shop.

Stewart's taste is simple but eclectic so one can count on the unpredictable. Nearly 75 percent of the merchandise is made up exclusively for his two stores.

Always on hand are hand-knitted Fair Isle sweaters at $225, and a year-round collection that many say has the best selection in the United States. Handsome carrying bags made in England out of Harris tweed cloth trimmed in leather ($225) are a specialty. You can also find garters at $5 a pair and suspenders at $12.

One hardly thinks of Woody Allen as a fashion plate, and yet he is a regular customer of Stewart Ross. On the other hand, so is Diana Ross. Stewart Ross has that kind of scope—from cotton chinos to high-class wearables.

SUSAN BENNIS/WARREN EDWARDS
440 PARK AVENUE
NEW YORK, N. Y. 10022
212/755-4197
MON.-FRI. 10-6:30, SAT. 10-6

Susan Bennis and Warren Edwards have been designing and producing uniquely styled shoes and boots for the past eight years, first under the Chelsea Cobbler logo, now under their own names. Their store has just moved to new, more spacious quarters on Park Avenue, splashing this stately street with the pink and mauve colors that dominate its new decor.

Bennis/Edwards shoes tend to have a similar effect on the viewer. They are definitely not for men (or women) who seek a classsic look in their clothes. Their men's shoes are high-styled and fashiony. Elegantly made in Italy by fine craftsmen, nevertheless there is always something distinctly different about Bennis/Edwards shoes. In many cases it is the leather. Bennis/Edwards like to use ostrich and wild boar skin, iguana and lizard. Or maybe it's the style itself, such as a pair of sneakers they did recently with lizard trim.

All Bennis/Edwards shoes are lined in leather and come with full leather soles. Quantities are limited, so the prices are high. A calfskin penny loafer with a smaller vamp than usual is $250. In ostrich the same shoe is $495.

Bennis/Edwards is for people who want to enjoy their shoes and don't mind paying for the pleasure. Many of the styles are eccentric, but a few qualify as long-term investments.

TENDER BUTTONS
143 EAST 62ND STREET
NEW YORK, N. Y. 10021
212/758-7004
MON.-FRI. 11-6, SAT. 11-5:30, EXCEPT JULY & AUG.

They say you can buy anything in New York, and Tender Buttons bears true witness to that claim. This charming shop sells only buttons. Begun thirteen years ago, it now houses the most complete collection of men's buttons in the world. There are English horn buttons from 45¢–$50, all colors of suit buttons, 200 types of blazer buttons. There are buttons for children and buttons for women, plastic buttons for a nickel apiece, enamel and diamonte buttons in a French set for $2000.

Diana Epstein and Millicent Safro, the owners, love buttons the way some people love old coins. They also love classical music, so you get both when you shop at Tender Buttons. If you are ever in need of that special shaped button, a gray horn beauty to match the other two left on your old tweed hunting jacket, this is the only place to look. If it doesn't have it, it probably doesn't exist anymore.

TRASH & VAUDEVILLE
4 St. Marks Place
New York, N. Y. 10003
212/674-9658
Mon.–Thurs. 12–8, Fri. 11:30–8, Sat. 11–8,
Sun. 1–6

Salespeople at this store answer the telephone with the salutation, "Hello, Trash," which pretty fairly captures the tone of irreverence that governs this store's mentality. Its new and used clothes are always slightly offbeat and humorous. Trash & Vaudeville was actually one of the first stores to do "punk" fashions, attracting such luminaries as Bette Midler and John Travolta.

The store began six years ago on the top floor of this address, but has since spread downstairs to the street level where it has arranged one of the most organized presentations of antique clothes anywhere. All items are displayed in oak and glass counters from the 1940's.

Trash & Vaudeville began as an antique clothing store of the 1940's and 1950's and this is where its strength remains. Its stock includes authentic rayon Hawaiian shirts from the fifties, $28–32, and silky rayon-gabardine shirts, $14–16. Of special interest is their extraordinary collection of embroidered gabardine cowboy shirts from the forties, many the famed H Bar C brand. These range from $35–40, and are a one-of-a-kind item, impossible to duplicate today.

VINCENT AND EDGAR
18 EAST 53RD STREET
NEW YORK, N. Y. 10022
212/753-3461
MON.-FRI. 9-5

Vincent and Edgar makes, without exaggeration, the most beautiful custom shoes I have ever seen. The lasts are exceptional, direct descendants of the elegantly shaped shoes of the 1930's and 1940's. The quality of the workmanship—the supple finishing of the leather, the small precise punching in the brogue designs—is as fine as one can possibly imagine.

Vincent and Edgar refers to the two Galvani brothers. Vincent is dead now and Edgar carries on by himself. Both brothers had a firm mastery of Italian craftsmanship. Their aesthetic, however, was English-American, which is what makes the shoes so special. In them are combined the best of both worlds—shoes with manly solidity that are pieced together with absolute delicacy.

The first pair of Galvani shoes costs $850. In the first four weeks a last is made and then a dummy leather shoe for the purchaser to sample. Vincent and Edgar is the only shoemaker in the world that actually makes a sample shoe. If any adjustments need to be made regarding the accuracy and comfort of the fit, they are made on it. The final shoe is made separately, completed six weeks after the sample shoe has been accepted.

The second pair of shoes, using the same last, costs $650 in standard leather. In Calcutta lizard the price is $1200.

These prices are undoubtedly high, but no one seeing a pair of Galvani shoes could deny their value.

WILLIAM FIORAVANTI, INC.
45 WEST 57TH STREET, 4TH FLOOR
NEW YORK, N. Y. 10019
212/355-1540
MON.-SAT. 8:30-5:30

You don't have to go to Rome to have a fine Italian suit made. Fifty-seventh Street is far enough. There, since 1951, in a showroom that looks as if it might have been transplanted from the Via Veneto, William Fioravanti has been producing superbly tailored suits and overcoats for many of New York's most important financial and corporate executives.

Behind the Italianate showroom, with its antique table and chairs, leather and tooled-gold walls, and Tiffany-style lamps, twenty-three tailors are constantly at work. Such a large staff permits Fioravanti to complete a suit in two weeks, if necessary, although the normal time is three months. Whatever the duration of its construction, though, each suit will be pieced together by hand and the linings will be pure silk.

A Fioravanti suit has a highly tailored look. The chest is clean, the waist suppressed and the sleeves narrowed. Fioravanti says his customers include "the guy who follows fashion as well as the guy who buys the same suit year after year." The majority appear to be the corporate exec type seeking an authoritative and powerful appearance.

Fioravanti suits start at $975, overcoats at $1000. Also available and in considerable demand by Fioravanti cutomers is a vicuna coat for $4800.

Philadelphia

PHILADELPHIA IS only ninety miles from New York City, and that has always been its greatest problem in nurturing fine men's clothing stores. The sophisticated Philadelphian generally chooses to shop in New York where clothes appear to be more exciting.

Of course Brooks Brothers has always done a fine business here. The Philadelphia lawyer or businessman, like his counterpart in Boston and Washington, is a responsible conservative stylist. Anything brighter than gray flannel is generally too bright for him.

For the other, more fashion-conscious man, shopping in Philadelphia continues to be somewhat of a problem. Some fine shops have opened in recent years, but surely not enough for this cultivated, wealthy city. Still one can only hope that the success of a store like Dimensions will encourage others to take the plunge. Then Philadelphians will no longer have to feel dependent upon New York to create a stylish wardrobe.

BARTON & DONALDSON
1635 CHANCELLOR STREET
PHILADELPHIA, PA. 19103
215/546-2324
MON.–FRI. 9–5

Barton & Donaldson, custom shirtmakers, just made *Philadelphia* magazine's Hall of Fame as one of the city's top furnishers, with good reason. They make the finest men's shirts in Philadelphia. Tucked into a little side street in the downtown section of the city, this twelve-year-old firm does all its own work on the premises. Each shirt is cut from an individual pattern by hand with a special short knife that guarantees meticulously clean lines. Shirts are made from imported cotton fabrics and only mother-of-pearl buttons are used. A four-shirt minimum order is required, and six to eight weeks delivery time. Shirts start at $50 apiece.

BROOKS BROTHERS
1500 CHESTNUT STREET
PHILADELPHIA, PA. 19102
215/564–4100
MON.–SAT. 9:30–5:30

See New York

DIMENSIONS
1627-29 CHESTNUT STREET
PHILADELPHIA, PA. 19103
215/564–1132
MON.–SAT. 9:30–5:30, WED. UNTIL 8:30

Dimensions is *the* store in Philadelphia for contemporary menswear. No store covers the ground it does, from Armani to Polo, from suits to underwear. New stores opening up locally feel, with justification, that Dimensions is their stiffest competition.

Founded in 1968 by Murray Korn, Dimensions began as a boutique selling mostly fashion merchandise. Korn felt this was the best way to attract the sophisticated Philadelphia buyer who in most cases was either shopping at Philly's Brooks Brothers branch or being lured into nearby New York for the more contemporary look. As the times changed Korn gave up the Nehru suit and other such fly-by-night articles and began to collect a more durable merchandise. Today his four-story shop with its stained glass windows and solid brass coat racks has a more traditional feel, though the general statement is still contemporary. Dimensions carries the natural-shoulder suits of Norman Hilton and Ralph Lauren. But it also carries the Italian looks of Armani and Zegna. These designer lines are supplemented by Korn's own finds and direct buys.

Prices here are moderate to expensive. Trousers are $70–200, sweaters $70–150, suits and jackets $185–500.

The staff is friendly and knowledgeable and there is an excellent tailoring shop on the second floor. Sales take place in January and July.

RODEO BEN TAILOR
6240 N. BROAD STREET
PHILADELPHIA, PA. 19141
215/924-4200
MON.–FRI. 10–5:30, WED. UNTIL 9, SAT. 10–5

This store is not what it once was when Ben was alive. Like the neighborhood that surrounds it, the shop has a dull run-down quality, with merchandise that is only mediocre. Yet Ben's son, now the store's owner, has knowledge of Western wear that few people today still possess. He used to accompany his father on the rodeo circuit, setting up shop in the towns where the cowboys were performing. From their hotel suite Rodeo Ben and Ben, Jr. would take orders and make up custom suits for all the cowboy stars.

Ben's son still has that capability. Press him and he'll make you an authentic Western-style rodeo suit in Forstmann wool gabardine. For $800 you can even have it with sequins.

Rodeo Ben Tailor invented the original denim Wrangler shirt, which one can see framed in the shop. It has had a strong effect on the country's current infatuation with Western wear. But today the shop seems almost more important as an historical monument than as a contemporary trend setter. However, if you have the desire for something really special, you can always approach Ben, Jr.

San Francisco

NEXT TO New York, San Francisco is the most sophisticated men's clothing city in the United States. It was here that the wearing of antique clothes began, and today its stylish used clothing stores are remarkable for both their number and diversity. But San Francisco also has a very strong traditional side. This side is nourished in part by the city's old elite, but also by the younger generation who in recent years have sought alternatives to the T-shirt-and-jean look.

The diversity of dress in San Francisco is a reflection of the diversity of the city itself, an amalgam of young professionals, old patrons and the most active gay community in the world. There is almost nothing you can't find in San Francisco if you look hard enough. It is what gives this city its charm as well as its strength.

ALL AMERICAN BOY
463 CASTRO STREET
SAN FRANCISCO, CALIF. 94114
415/861-0444
MON–SAT. 10–6.

This store primarily sells to San Francisco's large gay community. Its style of merchandise might best be described as ruggedly classic. Upon entering the store one gets the mistaken impression that this is a store primarily for "jocks." On display are all kinds of athletic body shirts and shorts, nylon track racing shorts ($10.00), satin basketball shorts ($10.00), Speedo racing swim suits ($8.50) and assorted styles of gym shorts ($5.50).

Many of the items in the store have All American Boy labels, but others are general classics: LaCoste cotton knit shirts in a myriad of colors ($21.50), web army belts in white, yellow, pink and gray ($4.50), cotton flannel shirts with flap pockets ($27.50–29.00), and the Levi's 501 button-front jean. The store employs two tailors full time to do alterations, especially on the jeans.

CABLE CAR CLOTHIERS/ROBERT KIRK LTD.
150 POST STREET
SAN FRANCISCO, CALIF. 94108
415/397-4740
MON.–SAT. 9:30–5:30

You cannot pick up a *New Yorker* magazine without noticing this store's striking advertisements, each one featuring one or more classic items available by mail. Such advertisements have undoubtedly broadened Cable Car's clientele, though its fine merchandise had long ago gained it a national following.

Founded in 1939 as San Francisco's sole outlet for British goods, it has in recent years marketed and sold merchandise made in all parts of the world. Even so the concept of Cable Car has not changed. Robert Kirk, its owner since 1973, insists on clothing and accessories of the finest quality, designed for the discriminating customer who leans toward a quiet, understated style.

The store is very much the archetype of America's image of a British clothing store. Plaid rugs, brass fixtures and a wooden winding stairway all contribute to its charming country-club atmosphere. Yet you do not have to visit the shop to enjoy its very special merchandise. Cable Car has an extensive brochure with full color reproductions of its merchandise. From that you can order almost any item a man might wear, from suit to underwear.

Suit prices begin at $235. A three-piece English gabardine suit is $365. Dress shirts start at $25. Silk rep ties are $15–18.50. A Harris tweed sport-jacket cut with a minimum of shaping sells for $195.

C. COOPER'S SHINE STAND
207 O'Farrell and Powell
San Francisco, Calif. 94102

There are no clothes sold here but $1.00 will get you a wonderful wax shoe shine and some interesting conversation as well. Both are provided by C. Cooper himself, who, after thirty-two years of shining shoes in this stand, is something of a San Francisco institution. Cooper knows half of San Francisco by name and his stall, with its Victorian-style pitched roof, is filled with photographs of the famous people who have been serviced by him. They include all the recent mayors of San Francisco, the Kennedys, and Bing Crosby, to name just a few.

Most shoes can use a good waxing, so if you're in the vicinity, stop by. A few minutes with C. Cooper will be remembered for a long time.

EDDIE BAUER
220 Post Street
San Francisco, Calif. 94108
415/986–7600
Mon.–Sat. 9:30–5:45, Thurs. until 6:30, Sun. 12–5

This store is part of a fourteen-store chain in the Far West that specializes in the sale of equipment and clothes for the outdoors. Founded in the 1930's, the store now carries an extensive line of goods, from sleeping bags to walking shorts, knapsacks, fishing rods, hip boots and binoculars. Its offerings fill a forty-eight-page catalogue sent out several times a year to customers throughout the country.

Bauer himself was a hiker, and he designed the first down parka for expedition purposes. This remains the store's real area of expertise—clothing and gear for backpacking and hiking. Stay away from the clothing for normal everyday wear. It is inexpensive but unexciting. Instead direct your attention to the fine selection of hiking shoes and boots ($69.00–82.50), parkas ($60.00 and up), foul-weather gear ($115.00), camouflage ponchos ($25.00), and down vests ($49.50).

OLD GOLD
2380 MARKET STREET
SAN FRANCISCO, CALIF. 94114
415/552–4788
MON.–SAT. 12–6

The sale of antique clothing in the United States really began in San Francisco, so it should not surprise anyone that this city can now boast of having the only used-clothing store in the world with a separate men's shop. Old Gold began like most, selling an agglomeration of used clothing, accessories, and jewelry—anything that was old and stylish—to anyone who was interested. Then as the store succeeded and grew, Dennis Mitchell and Joseph Dubois, the owners, began to think of themselves as a "department store of the past," separating their items into different sections. The final step was to separate the men's merchandise into its own store, just a block away from the original.

The men's shop carries used clothes and accessories from as far back as the 1920's, but its mainstay is the so-called classics of the 1950's. These include suits and jackets ($45 and up), and especially pleated trousers ($20 and up), Hawaiian shirts ($25–45), and an interesting selection of military gear. Mitchell and Dubois have good taste as well as excellent sources for their merchandise.

A Western-style tie clip from the 1950's found at Old Gold in San Francisco, $12.

While jewelry is only a small part of their business, they do maintain a wonderful collection of old tie clips, many with humorous designs. As tie clips were generally worn only by American men during the 1940's and 1950's (not by Europeans), they are difficult to locate. Yet somehow Old Gold invariably manages to keep a full stock on hand. Their prices range from $10 on up.

WILKES BASHFORD
336 SUTTER STREET
SAN FRANCISCO, CALIF. 94108
415/986-4380

Wilkes Bashford is one of the great newer stores in America. Like any unusual effort it is the product of one man's vision, in this case, Wilkes Bashford himself. Opening his store in 1966, Bashford decided that to succeed in sophisticated, wide open San Francisco he would have to cater to many tastes—the avant-garde, the classic American, the high-styled European. Rather than giving his store a personality through a specific style of clothes, he would do it by an unwavering standard of quality and service. His store has succeeded grandly, and with just that formula. Indeed the merchandise he sells is on a quality level unmatched in the United States.

The design of Wilkes Bashford is as much a part of Bashford's vision as the clothes. The entire floor has been divided into a series of closed spaces. This allows each style of dress to be isolated from the next and gives the customer a real sense of privacy and personal attention. Lots of space is left around each display so that customers can take notice and appreciate the hand-picked selections.

Some people might wonder whether it was incongruous to carry classic natural-shoulder suits and flashy avant-garde sportswear under one roof. To that Bashford replies that people need fantasy as well as the basics. I couldn't agree more.

For its classics Wilkes Bashford has a complete Ralph Lauren shop and carries Tommy Nutter hand-made suits from Savile Row ($1000). It also has an enormous quality shoe business. The sportswear is generally European and chosen with impeccable taste.

Prices are expensive here, as might be expected. In fact Wilkes Bashford is probably one of the most expensive stores in the country. Dress shirts start at $60, ties are $27.50 and up, suits $400 and up. But what you're buying here is not hype. This is the real thing—quality and service on a level almost unattainable in this day and age. Wilkes Bashford is for men who truly love fine clothes.

Washington

THIS CITY is a one-company town and that company
is the United States government. Its employees—politicians, bureaucrats, lawyers—take few chances that would raise an eyebrow. A gray suit is a Washington man's best friend.

There is some contemporary fashion here but the choice is small compared to cities like New York and Los Angeles. Look instead for fine quality
traditional wear—natural-shoulder suits, button-down-collar shirts, rep ties.
These clothes might not create much excitement, but then how many politicians do you know who do?

ARTHUR A. ADLER

5530 WISCONSIN AVENUE
CHEVY CHASE, MD. 20015
301/656-1505

1101 CONNECTICUT AVENUE N.W.
WASHINGTON, D.C. 20036
202/628-0131
MON.-SAT. 9:30-6

Arthur Adler began his career in the clothing business on the college
circuit. For several years he toured the universities and prep schools of the
Northeast taking suit orders from the wealthier students who would select
their materials from the swatches he carried in the back of his car. Then in
1943 he settled down in Washington and opened his own store.

Adler's success on the college circuit was predicated on the personalized service he offered each student. It is just such service that characterizes his shops today. No customer is ever harried into making a purchase.
And when a suit is selected it is fitted with the same care and attention to
detail that Adler offered forty years ago. No wonder so many of the city's
ambassadors and congressmen patronize his stores.

The clothing sold at Adler is updated traditional—geared to the university man who wants conservative styling with a bit of flair. The suits are
made by Southwick, Norman Hilton and Haspel—the quality manufacturers.
"We confine our buying to reputable manufacturers," says Adler. "If we
don't believe in them, we do not buy them." Adler is an Old Guard retailer

who seeks to be creative within a traditional mold. His two-piece wool suits sell for $265–450. Alden shoes, a fine quality make, are $95–135.

Adler has sales in January and June.

BRITCHES
1247 WISCONSIN AVENUE N.W.
WASHINGTON, D. C. 20007
202/338–3330
TUES.–SAT. 10–6, MON. UNTIL 9

Britches is part of a ten-store chain that sells only its own label suits and sportjackets. Their style is natural-shoulder, based roughly on the most recent Ralph Lauren designs. Yet because the firm's owners have the ability and taste level to act as their own designer/contractors, they are able to cut out the middle man. They go into the market themselves and buying in great quantities (for ten stores) are able to purchase quality materials and manufacture at reasonable prices. The end result is that they are able to offer the consumer considerable savings.

Three-piece wool suits, for instance, average $250. But there are also many at $195 and a few at $465. Shirts sell for $19.50–57.50, sweaters, $35–60.

Each of the Britches stores has a traditional clubby look with antique breakfronts, natural wood moldings and oriental rugs. The salesmen are young and eager to please. The clothing is not overly sophisticated, but a young man can feel safe buying there. He will get good value for his money and traditional clothing with some interest given to the styling.

THE DESIGNERS
WHITE FLINT MALL
KENSINGTON, MD. 20795
301/881–1900
MON.–FRI. 10–9:30, SAT. 10–6

This store is practically the only place in Washington where one can find fashion from Europe. Begun twelve years ago in Georgetown, The Designers recently moved into a new location where there is more room to show the broad spectrum of menswear lines owner Lawrence Savage enjoys selling.

The store has a clean modern look, a monochrome of gray extending from the carpeted floor to the painted walls which have been specially designed to display the separate collections of each designer. The store carries Jhane Barnes, Giorgio Armani, Pinky and Dianne and other quality designers who have an individual point-of-view.

Of special interest is The Designers' association with Lou Myles, a Canadian manufacturer. Through Myles The Designers is able to offer made-to-measure suits and shirts. A two-piece made-to-measure suit, which takes four to five weeks, costs $525. Made-to-measure shirts are $50–110. These prices are nearly competitive with the designer suits and shirts, yet men can choose to have them cut exactly the way they want rather than have a style and fit imposed upon them.

The Designers has sales on its ready-to-wear merchandise in January and June.

GEORGETOWN UNIVERSITY SHOP
36TH & N STREETS N.W.
WASHINGTON, D.C. 20007
202/337–8100
MON.–SAT. 9:30–5:45

The Georgetown University Shop looks exactly as one expects it to look and sells the kind of fine clothes one assumes university men would buy. The outside is the traditional Williamsburg brick front complete with mullioned windows. Inside are rich walnut moldings, Scotch plaid rugs and lovely framed prints of English pastoral and hunting scenes. The clothing is the basic Ivy League style—natural-shoulder suits, tweed sportjackets, button-down-collared shirts and bright colored sweaters.

The store was founded in 1908 by a football star at Georgetown University. In 1964 it was purchased by S. Thomas Saltz, a longtime dealer in the clothing business who has since authored more than 125 articles on menswear, all written under the byline, "Creative Retailers." Saltz carries no designer lines in the shop, but he has updated the traditional look somewhat by making sure the suits have subtly shaped silhouettes. These suits are made from fine quality English fabrics and are all hand-finished. The tailoring shop on the premises is expert in alterations.

Like many of the stores in Washington, the University Shop has had its share of famous clients—Lyndon Johnson, Robert Kennedy, George Bush, John Anderson, Hodding Carter. They have shopped here not only for suits, but for the store's fine selection of casual slacks ($50–100) and sportjackets ($185–250); for its button-down-collar shirts which are chosen from the top manufacturing lines ($25–40); and for the extensive collection of sweaters—

*The Irish Country Hat
from the Georgetown
University Shop,
Washington, D.C.,
$27.50.*

McGeorge shetlands and lambswools ($35–70), as well as the ruggedly beautiful Irish fisherman knits ($70) which are carried all year round.

The University Shop probably has the finest hat department in the United States. You can buy the best-made homburgs, fedoras, derbies, even top hats, though its most popular style at the moment is the Irish Country Hat ($27.50). This, Saltz proudly notes, the store sells more of than any other retail outfit in the country.

Washington is filled with stores selling traditional university-style clothes. The Georgetown University Shop was the first of its kind in the city and it remains the leader—a shop with wonderful personality and flavor.

Store-wide sales take place in January and July.

POLO
1220 CONNECTICUT AVENUE N.W.
WASHINGTON, D.C. 20036
202/463–7460
MON.–SAT. 10–6

This store represents the Ralph Lauren organization in Washington. Opened in the spring of 1980 in handsomely decorated quarters, it offers Lauren-designed clothing for men, women and children. The Lauren menswear line, practically unavailable here until now, will serve as an elegant complement to the tradition of natural-shoulder clothing that has so long typified Washington dress.

Suits start at $465.00, dress shirts $45.00–72.50, sweaters $65.00–185.00, ties $17.50–35.00.

7.
EUROPE

London

FOR THE well-dressed man looking to spruce up his wardrobe, there is no substitute for a stop in London. This medieval city on the Thames has more men's specialty shops per square inch than any other city in the world. Why this is so is not precisely clear though the explanation undoubtedly lies somewhere between the Englishman's love of tradition and the country's economics of rugged individualism.

At least since the time of Byron the English nobility have dictated men's fashions to the rest of the world. During Victorian times a gentleman's concern for the proper mode of attire became so extreme he was actually changing clothes five and six times a day, a practice much admired from afar though hardly ever duplicated. (A separate suit was donned for each meal, a different outfit for tea and for sport, and of course something special for those post-prandial walks and afternoon outings as well.) After World War I a more practical style of dress was introduced, heralded by the Duke of Windsor, who outraged London society the first time he wore a country suit in town. Yet withal the Englishman has never lost his fondness for dressing with distinction and individual flair, as a stop on any London street corner today will readily attest.

How in this age of mass-marketing he still manages to do so is a wonder of British economics. For somehow the country continues to support both tiny, individually owned shops and cottage-sized mills. The result is a near-paradise for the clothes-oriented man. Today in London there is an enormous variety of shops carrying men's clothes and furnishings, not to mention yards and yards of fine English cloth of a quality and diversity unobtainable elsewhere in the world, even in the United States. (Here the milling industry, like the meat industry, emphasizes the mass production of "choice" goods rather than a smaller output of prime.)

Men's fashion in London currently reflects 4 separate strains of influence. On Savile Row and Bond Street are the legendary "bespoke" tailors and men's furnishing shops—small handsome establishments which have been outfitting English gentlemen and most of the European nobility for more than fifty years. Here one can still find craftsmen trained in the Old World way offering quality and service to satisfy a man's every sartorial need. From hand-made shoes to the hand-sewn embroidered initials on his custom-made shirt, a man can delight in the experience of owning and wearing something made exclusively for him—clothes that fit his unique character, body and mind.

Out of contempt for the staid formality and traditionalism of the Savile Row tailors was born the excitement of Carnaby Street in the early 1960's. This excitement didn't last very long and when the street succumbed to economic pressures, the jean and T-shirt aesthetic found a new home on Kings Road, though what was once a symbol of rebellion has now become a kind of orthodoxy.

The third fashion influence appears to be a fusion candidate of the two competing parties, combining the quality and elegance of English fabric and tailoring with a more casual and contemporary design. The founding member of this group was a store called Browns, though others have quickly joined the fold. For the moment this style of contemporary elegance is perhaps the most significant force in English fashion.

Finally there exists throughout London an ever-changing group of young, innovative designers—recent graduates from the 3 major fashion schools—who design, produce and sell small collections of clothes that are exciting and wholly original. Though perhaps not to everyone's liking, these experimental designs are carefully watched by everyone in the men's fashion industry for the direction they might point to in the future.

If London has any drawback it is that it has too much to offer. A man can take days trying to decide what to purchase. Yet at any of the shops listed in this chapter he can count on the merchandise to have quality, durability and a strong sense of style, and even though prices have risen dramatically in the past two years, good value as well.

ACE

193 Kings Road, Chelsea
London SW 3
499–1469
Mon.–Sat. 9–6:30

This may be the "hottest" store in the world. There is nothing inside
here that does not glitter: the jeans, the shirts, the walls and the people.
Shopping here is like a night at Bond's—the black walls shine under silver
lights, music plays continuously, and there's no telling what stars may pop
in—Liza Minnelli, Rod Stewart, Bianca Jagger or the Rolling Stones.

Run by designer Peter Golding, this store on Kings Road has been
purveying its brand of funky elegance to London's party people since 1975.
Models, rock stars, movie people and lords and princesses come here for
clothes that Golding designs to be both fun *and* sexy. Famous are the Golding
jeans, which fit like a second skin. They come in cords and velvets of every
color, and for those really ready to take the plunge, in leather or with sequins
($75–150). Other items you might consider are one-of-a-kind T-shirts such as
those embroidered with rhinestones in the Honda or Harley-Davidson insig-
nia ($90). Ace also has interesting sequined sweatshirts and uniquely styled
sweaters ($100–225).

This is a unisex shop, so bring your wife or girlfriend. You'll find
yourself in the very best company.

*The ultimate T-shirt
designed by Peter
Golding of Ace, London;
100 percent cotton, hand-
embroidered with
rhinestones. An art to
wear classic, $75.*

ANDERSON & SHEPPARD
30 Savile Row
London W1
734–1420
Mon.–Fri. 8:30–5

In the 1930's Douglas Fairbanks, Jr., Fred Astaire and Rudolph Valentino had more in common than the idolatry of the American woman. Each of them loved Anderson and Sheppard clothes. Like Michael Arlen who introduced Valentino to the shop, and Diaghilev who flew in from Paris for fittings, they all came for the uniquely soft-styled design, an original blending of tailored elegance with sportswear casualness.

The Anderson and Sheppard style continues to be unique on Savile Row in its achievement of elegance through softness instead of by the severity of line. It is the true inheritor of the famous 1930's "drape suit" which had broader shoulders and nipped-in waist. The suit jacket, rather than being stiff and form-fitting, sits comfortably on the shoulders without padding and high armholes. The pleated pants are broad but shaped along the legs, and hang straight with cuffs. The four-pocket vest sits with its bottom button permanently open. The overall effect is one of casual, lived-in elegance.

Apart from the distinct styling of an Anderson and Sheppard coat or suit (the tailors will actually create any design you ask them though it seems a

Sheepskin-lined suede slippers from Anderson & Sheppard, London. Under the turned-down lip is a cord which protects against stretching, $35.

Trousers by Anderson &
Sheppard, London. These
custom-made slacks are
made especially to be
worn with suspenders
with a curved back and
adjustable belt, $200.

shame to waste their particular talents), it is worth visiting the shop if only for the marvelous selection of fabrics. It maintains probably the best selection in London—stripes, tweeds, glen plaids and herringbones, of all hues and textures. Many of these exclusive fabrics duplicate those used in the 1920's and 1930's though they are a lighter weight. The formal wear cloth is particularly choice—mohairs and baratheas with etched-in stripes and herringbones.

Prices are fairly reasonable for fine custom tailoring. Two-piece suits start at $800, three-piece suits from $900. Odd trousers are $250, overcoats $750, formal attire $1,000. A first fitting generally takes two weeks. Several weeks later the completed garment can be mailed home. Ask Mr. Halsey to help you with fabric selection. For design and cutting, request Mr. Halbrey.

To match the soft look of its suits Anderson & Sheppard carries an entirely unique collection of cashmere ties. These are cut 3½ inches wide and come in a broad variety of colors and patterns—solids, plaids, tick weaves and herringbones. *Warning!* If you've never worn cashmere ties, be careful. They can be addictive, and their cost is $22.50 apiece.

For softness at home, try the sheepskin-lined moccasins. For a mere $35 your feet can stay warm all through the winter.

AQUASCUTUM
100 REGENT STREET
LONDON W1
734–6090
MON.–SAT. 9–5:30, THURS. UNTIL 7

Aquascutum has the largest selection of ready-to-wear topcoats and raincoats in London, if not in the world. It also carries suits, velvet jackets and tuxedos. But it is the outerwear that since 1851 has brought Aquascutum worldwide recognition, and it is to this department that I would generally confine my buying.

The Aquascutum coat is made completely in the company's own factory. The quality of the workmanship is matched only by the quality of the materials: luxurious cashmere spun and woven in Scotland, pure English lambswool and exclusive tweeds, all created and milled specially for Aquascutum. The styles of coats are numerous. They include fine traditional double-breasted tweed overcoats, Chesterfields in single- or double-breasted, rich fur collar evening coats, and of course, the famous Aquascutum trench coat, with or without removable wool or cashmere lining. The breadth of sizes on hand is truly remarkable: from 36 extra-short to 50 long—2000 coats in stock.

Aquascutum coats are expensive, but they are an investment, and they will offer a fine and lasting return.

Wool melton overcoats are $400, camelhair $800, cashmere $1000. The raincoats start at $375 in poly-cotton.

ARMOUR-WINSTON LTD.
43 BURLINGTON ARCADE
LONDON W1
493–8937
MON.–FRI. 9–5

This beautiful little shop specializes in men's vintage jewelry. The owners buy large estates and save the most interesting pieces for their own customers.

The shop itself is one of the most handsome in the arcade, with a true Edwardian feeling. There are highly polished chevron wood floors, velvet chairs, and a large antique tapestry hanging on the back wall. Inside the display cases is one of the more extensive stocks of old cuff links in London, some dating from before the turn of the century. These start at $140 a pair. Not long ago Armour-Winston was selling a set of 1940's cuff links from Cartier. Made out of 18-karat gold in the shape of a golf ball and tee, their price was $600, which was expensive, but less than the cost of an ounce of gold today. The shop also carries men's studs, rings and an occasional tie pin.

BEALE & INMAN LTD.
131 NEW BOND STREET
LONDON W1
629–4723
MON.–FRI. 9–5, SAT. 9–12:30

In 1972 an American newspaper columnist wrote about Beale & Inman:

Of all our favourite shops abroad perhaps Beale & Inman at 131 New Bond Street, London, is our favourite. . . . Napoleon shopped there, it

Silk-lined, hand-stitched hogskin gloves. The finest gloves available today. Beale & Inman Ltd., London, $70.

All-wool, hand-framed socks from Beale & Inman, London. Available by mail in twenty different shades with initials in any contrasting color. A great gift item, $20.

was in the first London directory in 1830, a cheque from Charles Dickens, framed, testified he spent 34 pounds 5 shillings there in 1859, and the flavour of the quiet, old-fashioned premises is so very English you expect Bob Cratchit to present the bill.

The description is as apt today as it is likely to be ten years from now. The world changes, but Beale & Inman somehow manages to continue in its own remarkable way. As they say in their own brochure, "In these days of mergers and takeovers, it is rather unusual to learn of a business still trading as a family concern after 150 years. Our Governing Director is Mr. Victor Inman, a grandson of Mr. Richard Inman, who was the first of the family to be associated with the company."

Beale & Inman is the one-stop furnishings establishment in London nonpareil. Everything it carries is made from only natural fibers, styled and crafted in the finest Old World tradition.

Its custom-made shirts are the best in London. They are finished by hand with special shoulder seams that allow for lengthening of the sleeves should the size of the shirt or your arms change. Its selection of fabrics is broad and uniquely English in style, while its salesmen and fitters are unsurpassed in knowledge of their craft. All this combined makes buying and wearing a Beale & Inman shirt a very special experience. Cotton shirts are $92.50 each with a three-shirt order required.

The shop also carries London's largest and most diverse selection of hose. These come in all sizes and fabrics, from cashmere to cotton lisle. You can even have socks with your initials ($22.50). Beale & Inman hand-finished gloves start at $60; their underwear in silk, wool, cotton or Swiss voile ranges from $12–50.

Unfortunately there are never any sales at Beale & Inman. But then, how can one discount a tradition?

BOWRING, ARUNDEL & COMPANY
31 SAVILE ROW
LONDON W1
629–8745
MON.–FRI. 8:30–5

In the movie *Pat and Mike* Spencer Tracy characterizes Katharine Hepburn with a description that might aptly be applied to Bowring, Arundel: "There may not be much meat on her, but what there is is choice." Tucked into the side of Anderson & Sheppard on Savile Row, this shop is one of the smallest in London, and yet its collection of men's furnishings is probably the most distinctive in the city. Its selection of indivdual items may not always be all-encompassing but whatever it sells is of the finest quality and styled with impeccable taste.

Established in 1860, Bowring, Arundel continues to believe business can be carried on in the "old way." This means it will custom-make ties and suspenders, the only shop in London to still do so. It also employs two of the

Three distinctive ties from the finest collection of English ties in the world at Bowring, Arundel & Company, London, $27.50.

English silk wedding ties from Bowring, Arundel, London, $24.

only five remaining women in England who sew shirt buttonholes by hand. (The other three are at Beale & Inman.) The "old way" also means plenty of service to the customer. The three staff members are most congenial and will spend hours discussing their merchandise with both patience and good humor. It is open during lunch hours and will deliver your packages free of charge to your residence or hotel.

Because everyone here is so patient, Bowring, Arundel is probably the best store in London in which to have shirts made for the first time. The salesmen will help you select fabrics and collar styles. And if you want something original—a special design notation or collar shape—they are more than willing to oblige. The shop's performance record in realizing just what you've envisioned has almost no equal. Its shirts rarely disappoint. Fabrics come in a fine selection of English and Swiss cottons and silks. Cost is $85 apiece with a minimum of three shirts required. Delivery time is three to five weeks depending on the season.

Bowring, Arundel has without a doubt the best selection of English-type ties in London. These are 3¼ inches in width and can be narrowed if desired. There are no prints here; every design is woven into the tie. In addition to an exclusive collection of striped regimentals ($25) the shop carries shepherd checks and lace weave silks for dress that are unique ($27); as well as occasional old ties it has managed to find with special sporting motifs in traditional country hues. It will custom-make any of its regimental stripes into bow ties or will make up four-in-hands or bows with fabric you supply. It will also order made-to-measure suspenders if the supplier is so inclined that day. Custom-made ties start at $22; suspenders, $17–25.

Lastly this shop sells as fine a quality handkerchief as can be bought in London. A special group of white linens come with hand-rolled edges in contrasting colors of burgundy, navy or brown ($10).

BRIAN & LYNN HOLMES
GRAY'S ANTIQUE MARKET
58 DAVIES STREET
LONDON W1
629–7327
MON.–FRI. 10–6

Brian & Lynn Holmes occupies one of fifty or so stalls that comprise Gray's Antique Market, an indoor shopping pavilion where one can spend hours enjoyably browsing. Each stall in Gray's specializes in one sort of antique or collectible. The Holmeses, who have been in business for ten years, sell fine old jewelry.

If you are looking for men's cuff links from the 1920's and 1930's, they have a large collection ranging in price from $85 for pewter to $2500 for diamonds. They also stock signet rings and antique men's wedding bands. Considering how scarce men's bands are today, their large supply is always a pleasurable mystery. They are priced from $140–600. Even scarcer at the moment are Edwardian tie clips. These they have only from time to time. When you can find one, it is, at $150, as excellent an investment as it is fun to wear.

Collectible Victoriana.
Eighteen-karat gold antique
cuff links from Brian & Lynn
Holmes, Gray's Antique
Market, London, $275.

BROWNS
23 SOUTH MOLTON STREET
LONDON W1
491–7833
MON.–WED. & FRI. 10–6, THURS. UNTIL 7, SAT. 10–5

When Browns first opened its doors nine years ago, it gave a shot to the men's fashion industry heard round the world. For the first time a grouping of contemporary men's clothes and furnishings was presented in the spirit of a collection. Simon Burstein and his associate designers had a point-of-view about fashion and that statement was expressed in all aspects of the shop's merchandise—in its suits, jackets, shirts, sweaters, ties, shoes and outerwear. Of course had that point-of-view not been right for the times, the shop might have died on the vine. But as things turned out, the look of casual English elegance, a kind of crumpled chic, became part of the major fashion movement of the decade.

Today Browns is a London institution, not just a store but a way of life. There is a Browns shop for women's clothes, a Browns shoe shop, a Molton Brown restaurant and a Molton Brown hair salon for both men and women. Each of them embodies the original Browns philosophy, a concern for style and elegance that is not contrived or fussy but which reflects the casualness and natural living style of our times.

Recently Browns has begun to distribute a ready-to-wear line worldwide. (It is carried by Barney's in New York.) But seeing these reproductions is no substitute for a visit to the original. The store itself is one of the handsomest in London with green plants and modern furniture played against an impressive array of Old World trappings. More important many of the interesting items on sale are never shipped abroad. They are made up specially for the shop in small quantities and disappear off the shelves almost as soon as they are set out. Many of these articles have been made by English designers, but an equal number come from the young Continental designers the shop is always cultivating. (Browns actually featured Giorgio Armani and Walter Albini before they were recognized in their home country of Italy. And its collection of Cerruti sportswear continues to be better presented than in the designer's own store in Paris.)

Browns' suits and topcoats are an updated version of traditional English tailored clothing. Using classic British fabrics it creates suits and coats with a looser more casual appearance. These are clothes for easy living, a country look that feels right in town. Suits start at $325, topcoats at $260.

The shoes are of a similar cast. They are updated versions of British classics. Bench-made in England of high quality leather and suede, they are serious with just the right touch of humor. Prices start at $70.

Because so much of what the store carries changes from month to month, it is difficult to recommend any one specific article of sportswear. However for the winter you can always count on an excellent collection of corduroy and flannel trousers ($85). In the summer these trousers are made up in linen and cottons ($65). Look also for marvelous shirts, easy fitting and contemporary in design, but manufactured out of traditional English fabrics— tattersalls, checks and fine stripings ($65-135). Browns sells as well fine English wool sweaters and interesting outerwear: rubberized raincoats ($140), sporty topcoats ($300) and reversible jackets ($150).

COLES
33 SAVILE ROW
LONDON W1
434-1290
MON.–FRI. 9-5:30, SAT. 9–1

This 100-year-old shop, three shops down from Bowring, Arundel on Savile Row and not much larger than a matchbox, could probably only exist and continue to flourish in a city like London. It is essentially a shirt shop, but what gives Coles its particular British air is the fact that it sells separate stiff collars. Not just a few, mind you, but literally hundreds each month. Indeed Coles has the widest range of celluloid collars in the world, styles varying from the very formal wing collar to the more standard straight-pointed collar. Ralph Lauren's English cutaway collar was actually based on one of the models here.

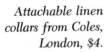

Attachable linen collars from Coles, London, $4.

These detachable collars, which used to be part of every man's dress, are now almost an anachronism. But Coles keeps selling and the British continue to buy. At $4 apiece, they can make a man look his elegant best.

FORSTER & CO.
16 CLIFFORD STREET
LONDON W1
734–2248
MON.–FRI. 9:15–5:15, SAT. 9:30–12:30

This is one of London's old tailoring firms, but rather than its tailored clothing, it is sweaters that make Forster special. Curiously in addition to its own tailoring shop, Forster owns a knitwear house that manufactures hand-knit, wool cable sweaters in authentic English club colors and stripings. If you are a foreigner and will be exporting the sweater, it will sell to you. Otherwise you must show your club membership before a club sweater leaves the premises.

At least twenty different color combinations are in stock at any one

The original cricket or tennis sweater from Forster & Co., London. This sweater is 100 percent wool and made with hand-knitted cables. Available in a wide selection of club colors. Beenies, braces and ties are sold in matching club stripes, $72.

time. Others are available on a seasonal basis. At $70 for a long-sleeved sweater and $60 for the short-sleeved V-neck, these are some of London's best values. The ultimate tennis sweaters!

Forster also carries suspenders, caps and ties to match the club sweaters. Suspenders and caps are $17, ties $14.

GIEVES & HAWKES LTD.
1 Savile Row
London W1
434–2001
Mon.–Fri. 9–5:30, Sat. 9–1

Gieves & Hawkes was formerly one of the most prestigious custom tailors on Savile Row. It still makes military uniforms for the Royal family, but today its real area of specialty is the ready-made suit. If you want a ready-made English-cut suit, the Gieves & Hawkes' models from Chester Barrie are the finest in London. They have been called the Rolls-Royce of ready-made suits.

Each Chester Barrie suit is made 70 percent by hand. Every suit is hand-cut individually and sewn together with 10,000 hand stitches. At Gieves & Hawkes the alterations are done by custom tailors.

Chester Barrie suits come in only a small selection of styles. But perhaps more important they are available in a large range of fittings—189 in all. This means the customer has an excellent chance of having his suit end up looking like it was custom-made on his body. In fine woolen fabrics, two-piece suits cost about $475.

HENRY MAXWELL & CO.
11 Savile Row
London W1
734–7441
Mon.–Fri. 9–6

"Behind the doors of Henry Maxwell & Co., bootmakers and spurriers, lies a timeless world of officers and gentlemen, patent pumps and spats, and a green, green England where the Port is always vintage and the hunting fields stretch on forever. The feeling of security reflects Maxwell's insistence on maintaining standards of craftsmanship, excellence and service that have largely disappeared elsewhere. . . ."

This description was published in the 1978 *Fashion Guide to London*. And though Maxwell continues to produce excellently made shoes, one's feeling of security about it has been undermined by the fact that it has been forced to move from its sumptuous quarters on New Bond Street to a small basement shop on Savile Row. Clearly the shop is not what it used to be when one practically needed a personal invitation to have shoes made there. Indeed a display case of models made years ago is more inspiring than what one sees now.

But Maxwell can still turn out some fine footwear, though their new prices are making that pleasure increasingly dear. Specialties include tasseled slip-ons ($650); full brogues with long, pointed wing-tips ($700); monogrammed velvet slippers ($550); and riding boots in waxed calf ($2000).

In addition Maxwell carries one of the largest selections of spurs in the world; it also stocks ready-to-wear shoes, leather goods and accessories, a fine collection of drink cases, riding crops and items like deerbone boot hooks and boot jacks for its equestrian enthusiasts.

Made-to-measure shoes require two months for delivery.

HENRY POOLE & COMPANY
10-12 CORK STREET
LONDON W1
734-5985
MON.–FRI. 9–5:30, SAT. 9–12:30

Poole & Company is the world's oldest and probably most famous men's tailor. Founded in 1806, it received its first royal warrant of appointment from Emperor Napoleon III in the 1840's. Thereafter it furnished the wardrobes for most of Europe's and Asia's nobility, including royal representatives from Russia, Prussia, Persia, Japan, Ethiopia, Egypt, and of course, England.

Today the company's clientele is perhaps not so majestic, but they still comprise some of the world's smartest dressers. They come to Poole for suits made from the finest British woolens—Huddersfield worsteds, Scottish tweeds, West-of-England flannels—sewn and fitted in the firm's century-and-a-half-old tradition of quality and craft. It is Poole's aim to adapt clothing to a customer's taste and body configuration, rather than to impose a rigid "house style." Its suits have evolved with the times but they make a point of not exaggerating stylistic details. For as is said at the shop, "A Henry Poole suit must not be a short-lived creation but remain always in good taste." It has managed to do this for 150 years. I have no doubt the next 150 will be equally successful.

A two-piece Poole suit begins at $950, topcoats at $720, formal suits $1275 with vest or cummerbund.

Poole originated the traditional connection of Savile Row with the best in men's tailoring, but in 1961 the firm was forced to leave the Row when redevelopment led to the demolition of their building. Installed on Cork Street now, its new headquarters has none of the nineteenth-century charm of the original, though fortunately the company did manage to incorporate some of the impressive original furniture from the earlier Poole. One piece of particular interest is a leather chair that is actually a scale for checking your change in weight from one fitting to the next.

H. HUNTSMAN & SON
11 SAVILE ROW
LONDON W1
734-7441
MON.–FRI. 9–1, 2–6; SAT. 9–12

If the name isn't enough to remind you that this prestigious establishment makes some of the finest riding clothes in the world, the fitting rooms certainly will. Each one contains a properly saddled wooden horse so that customers can be assured of a perfect fit of their riding habits. But equestrian garb is only a portion of the Huntsman business. Any firm that has gained a reputation for making fashionable attire which not only lasts but continues to look well under the harshest conditions of the hunt can obviously be counted on to produce a well-made suit. And in this field Huntsman has secured itself a reputation of equal standing.

There are, in fact, many in the know who consider Huntsman the finest men's tailor in London. It certainly is the most expensive. A Huntsman three-piece wool suit will cost almost $650 more than those of its competitors. Whether this supererogation is justified is not a simple question to answer. Even to the educated eye there is nothing that particularly distinguishes a Huntsman suit from those produced by other fine Savile Row tailors. They are all traditionally styled, padded and shaped by hand to sleekly clothe the body. Nor did an hour's conversation with the Huntsman staff convince me there was anything so extraordinary in their tailoring methods as to account for the broad discrepancy in price.

Yet English tailors can be as crafty as French chefs in their refusal to divulge their product's most important ingredients. And in all fairness to the firm there is an atmosphere of precision and meticulous concern in the cutting and sewing rooms the likes of which exist nowhere else in London. One can believe that no stitch will be dropped, no button will ever fall off. Such exacting care takes time and a Huntsman suit requires five separate fittings (most tailors suggest two) and a ten-to-twelve-week delivery time. Still, Huntsman customers—and they are legion—don't seem to mind the extra wait or cost. Great things, they say, are worth waiting and paying for.

Like a number of other Savile Row tailors Huntsman uses fabrics made up exclusively for the shop. Of particular interest are the heavy tweeds which are milled in limited editions and provide only enough material for ten garments. Designed for English hunt coats, they are too heavy for indoors but ideal for use in men's topcoats. These cost approximately $1400. Two-piece suits start at $1800 in wool, $2000 in silk. Three-piece suits are $60 more. The prices are stratospheric but if the garment carries a Huntsman label, you can be sure of unsurpassable quality, both in materials and workmanship.

In addition to tailored clothing Huntsman carries some other items of interest. The traditional English riding shirt, knitted in wool but with a woven collar band to which a separate stiff collar may be attached, is here carried in a luscious cashmere ($100). It is the ultimate in country elegance, worn as a collarless shirt or as a sweater.

There is also an unusual collection of enameled jewelry with various horse motifs. These come in tie clips ($125); cuff links ($750) and links and studs ($850). All trim is 18-karat gold.

A broad selection of classic English belts is carried in precious skins—alligator, ostrich, pigskin and lizard—with plated gold and silver buckles. Prices start at $65.

Lastly there are the Huntsman handkerchiefs. Like most articles sold here these are twice the price of anyone else's. The quality, however, is unrivaled anywhere in the world. The hand-rolled Irish linens woven exclusively for the shop, are as soft as the finest silk. And they come in two-tone combinations that are a unique Huntsman inspiration—beige with dark gray trim; pink with gray; green with a darker green. It is impossible to overrate these marvels of handiwork, but at $13.50 apiece they are a sheer luxury.

HOWIE
138 Longacre
London, WC2
240-1541
Mon.–Fri. 10–6:30, Sat. 10–6

Paul Howie and his wife, Lynn, entered the clothing business ten years ago with a splash, carrying way-out, avant-garde styles that soon became all the rage. Now they have settled down somewhat, and the emphasis is on quality classics. The treatment, of course, is not like Savile Row; it is classicism infused with great, funky imagination: wonderful cotton and silk shirts, deep-pleated trousers, jackets of fine English fabrics, all in marvelously bright colors. This shop specializes in women's clothes, but the downstairs men's shop always carries interesting sportswear. Howie is linked up with lots of the young fashion shops in Europe and new things come in all the time. The taste is rarely eccentric. Nevertheless this is a shop with its hand on the pulse of the fashion moment. Shirts start at $50, trousers $75–125, jackets $185–250.

J. C. CORDING & COMPANY LTD.
19 PICCADILLY
LONDON W1
734–0830
MON.–FRI. 9–5

Since the nineteenth century Cording has been recognized in both England and abroad as a retailer of top quality raincoats, riding mackintoshes, shooting clothing and outdoor footwear. Established in 1839 at the old Temple Bar in the Strand in the City of London, this historic firm carries

Barbour jacket made from thorn-proof waxed cotton. The original jacket from England for fishing or shooting, $95.

almost everything for the outdoor activist. The three-story shop, located just a stone's throw away from Piccadilly Circus, is a pleasure to browse through, filled with classic and unusual merchandise from shooting stockings to loden capes, from Harris tweed breeches to Norfolk jackets and Moorland coats made of handsome Yorkshire tweed.

Cording specializes in garments made of Grenfell cloth. This material, named after Sir Wilfred Grenfell, the doctor-explorer, was originally made to protect him on his explorations of the Arctic. Since then it has been used whenever a high performance, light cotton material was essential, on five Mt. Everest expeditions and by many Olympic ski teams. Golf jackets in Grenfell are $125. Anoraks for climbing or casual wear cost $165; double-breasted trench coats are $240.

Another weatherproofed item worth investigating is the Barbour gamefair jacket. This is a super-light over-jacket for shooting and hunting. Like its companion jacket, the Barbour Durham, it is made of unlined oilskin-type fabric, and comes with Belbour pockets, a lined collar and adjustable inside wind cuffs. Both jackets come only in olive color, and cost $85.

Though Cording does little custom work any more, they will, upon request, make up an English covert cloth coat with velvet collar, complete with the traditional rows of stitching around the bottom. This coat at $275 is excellent value. Like most Cording merchandise, it is a "classic" and one can count on wearing it in style indefinitely.

JOHN LOBB
9 St. James's Street
London W1
930–3664/5
Mon.–Fri. 9–5:30, Sat. 9–1

John Lobb is probably the most famous shoemaker in the world. Founded in 1829, it has serviced at one time or another most of Europe's royalty, and today holds royal warrants from both the Duke of Edinburgh and Queen Elizabeth II. The store itself is a kind of working museum, unchanged since the 19th century, everything slightly worn and smelling of leather. A sense of history abounds from the manner and dress of the salesmen to the display of original shoes made by the shop 150 years ago.

Lobb's shoes used to be considered without peer, but in recent years the firm has lost many of its older workmen and the product has suffered. It is still an excellently hand-crafted shoe, but in my opinion it doesn't quite compare to the shoes made by Lobb, Paris, its French brother. The London shop, in addition, is too inflexible about styling. It wants the shoe to look the way it wants, and it also wants six months to make it.

None of this seems to have affected the Lobb business however. A Lobb customer is a customer for life. He knows he can count on a sturdily made shoe of the best leather and service with 19th century care and concern.

Shoes in calf leather start at $700 a pair, in alligator or crocodile, $2000. Boots are $1150.

LLOYD-JENNINGS
54-56 NEAL STREET, COVENT GARDEN
LONDON WC2
836–8906
MON.–SAT. 10–6
6 BOW LANE
LONDON
836–8906
MON.–FRI. 9–6

This firm is only three years old, though its clientele and merchandise would lead one to think otherwise. In a short period of time Lloyd-Jennings has managed to attract a wide following of traditional customers, many from the financial district, and many who previously had purchased only custom-made shoes. They come here for a selection of ready-made shoes that have all the appearance of bespoke shoes of the past, and for a fraction of the cost.

The owners of Lloyd-Jennings recognized several years ago that the prices of custom-made shoes were fast rising into the stratosphere. Obviously not all the customers of Lobb and Maxwell would be able to stay aboard. They decided then to copy the lasts of these great shoemakers and manufacture them in wholesale quantities. This is what they did, and today Lloyd-Jennings is an ensured success. Indeed the firm has already opened a second store in the financial district and will soon be opening a third.

Lloyd-Jennings shoes are really for men who appreciate the lightness and quality of a fine bench-made shoe, but who cannot afford to have them custom-made. The shop carries a good range of styles, all classic English models, each made from the finest leathers. Its prices vary between $100 and $275 a pair.

Lloyd-Jennings has an excellent repair service. It also offers a fine ready-to-wear riding boot that is every bit as good as the one made by Maxwell, but costs ⅓ the price. Made from the same quality skin, available in a selection of heights, calf widths and insteps, it is $800. Boot trees are $240.

LOCK & CO.

6 St. James's Street
London SW1
930–8874
Mon.–Fri. 9–5, Sat. 9:30–12:30

There are few old firms in London that cannot attach themselves to a piece of history, but Lock & Co. may very well have the largest claim. This noble firm sent Nelson to Trafalgar in a hat with a specially fitted eyepiece, supplied the hat that Wellington wore at Waterloo, made Oscar Wilde a floppy velvet hat to go with his knickerbocker suit, and presented England with its first bowler. You can still find the classic tophats and bowlers here, called "Coke hats" in memory of the client for whom they were first made, but Lock & Co. also carries a large selection of leisure hats. Occupying this same shop since 1765, the firm now carries golf caps, riding hats, trilbys and deerstalkers—the Sherlock Holmes model. All hats are available in ready-to-wear or made-to-measure. Lock retains individual measurements and records of transactions so you can write them for replacements year after year.

Bowlers in hard fur felt start at $85, town-and-country lightweight trilbys at $58, and deerstalker hats with or without ear flaps at $45.

For made-to-measure add an additional $15 and allow for a three-month delivery.

LORD'S

Burlington Arcade
London W1
493–5808
Mon.–Fri. 9–5:15, Sat. 9–1

Lord's is the oldest shop in the Burlington Arcade and for many years was *the* men's furnishings shop in London. Built around the turn of the century, it remains a stunning example of Victoriana, with its gleaming walnut

Hand-finished, cashmere-and-silk scarf with silk fringe. The height of versatility and opulence. Lord's, London, $90.

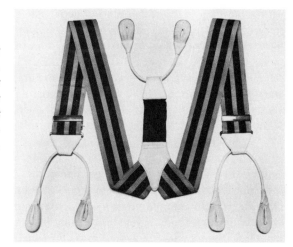

Suspenders from Lord's in Burlington Arcade, London. These are the old-style braces made with white calf-gut trimmings that are hand-finished, $27.50.

display cabinets and plush red velvet interior. On the walls are photographs of Winston Churchill and Anthony Eden, once two of the firm's more illustrious clients.

The shop carries a varied selection of merchandise, sweaters and robes on the second floor at the top of a winding staircase, suspenders, gloves and scarves on the first floor. The sweaters and robes are of fine quality, but it is the downstairs merchandise that is particularly distinctive. Look for the beautiful cashmere scarves, $60, or for great versatility and elegance, scarves made of silk on one side, cashmere on the other, $95. Lord's gloves come in an endless variety of leathers and styles, from pigskin to calf, doeskin and chamois, $50–80. The shop also carries the best selection of suspenders in London, in an amazing array of stripes and solids, for casual wear or formal attire, $27.50.

MOSS BROS
26 BEDFORD STREET, COVENT GARDEN
LONDON WC2
240-4567
MON.–FRI. 9–5:30, THURS. UNTIL 7, SAT. 9–1

This is the type of store one likes to spend time browsing through, full of interesting corners and surprises. Moss Bros seems to carry a little bit of everything English, from its tailoring department which offers made-to-measure shirts, suits and military uniforms at extremely reasonable prices, to its livery department which outfits chauffeurs, porters and waiters. Moss Bros pioneered quality ready-to-wear clothes in England and it has a huge selection for both casual and dress wear. It also maintains one of the biggest riding and saddlery departments in the world, complete with riding jackets and scarlet evening dress coats, breeches, jodhpurs, saddles, bridles and polo wear.

But of all its departments, it is Moss Bros' rental service that has gained the store almost international recognition. On a moment's notice Moss Bros can provide peers' robes, velvet court suits, military uniforms, morning suits and top hats, tailcoats, opera cloaks, Highland dress, and a myriad of other items from cummerbunds to shoes and spats. You can hire these items for a day, week or month, or you can buy them new. You can also purchase them from the rental stock at substantially reduced prices, which may be one of the best bargains in London. The following are sample rental prices: cutaway and trousers, $38.00; accessories, $12.00; opera cloak, $36.00; scarf, $3.50; formal shoes, $6.50. If it is something English you want and you can't find it elsewhere, try Moss Bros. The prices are always right and the service dependable.

NEW & LINGWOOD
53 JERMYN STREET
LONDON SW1
493-9621
MON.–FRI. 9–5:30, SAT. 9–12:30

New & Lingwood is one of London's great traditional men's furnishing shops. Don't look for the latest fashions here. This is the only store in the world where the salesmen still dress in shirts with separate white stiff collars. The clientele of New & Lingwood is old and highborn. The shop even has a special branch on the campus of Eton.

With such accreditation one would expect high quality, and that's precisely what is found here: hosiery made of the finest wool and cotton lisles for $7–20; silk robes, fine spun cotton underwear and elegant suspenders. Its selection of traditional English ties is one of the largest in London—beautiful polka dots, stripes and foulards. These ties are a good width for today at 3¼ inches; they range in price from $20–30.

The shirt department at New & Lingwood is also quite extensive. They offer a profusion of models in cotton ($45–65), and perhaps the greatest selection of shirts with detachable collars in the world. These are available in stripes or solids, in Sea Island cottons or voiles. Their $68 price includes a choice of two separate soft collars.

POULSEN & SKONE
53 JERMYN STREET
LONDON SW1
493–9621
MON.–FRI. 9–5:30, SAT. 9–12:30

There is nothing particularly distinctive about the look of this small shop, upstairs from the fine men's furnishings firm of New & Lingwood. But Poulsen & Skone today makes probably the finest custom-made shoe in London. It is certainly the least expensive and can be delivered the quickest.

In recent years, as some of the fine old workers have left Maxwell, they have resumed employment with Poulsen & Skone. Among these was George Cleaverly, who at eighty-one years old is the dean of London's shoe makers. Cleaverly's grandfather made shoes, as did his father who worked for John Lobb. Cleaverly himself is a legend in the trade, having designed and made shoes for over sixty years, his clients including Churchill, Eisenhower,

The original slipper made for the Eton School by Poulsen & Skone, London, in 1865. Available in navy, burgundy, green or black corduroy. All come trimmed with black leather, $60.

*The original chukka boot,
made by Poulsen & Skone
for over fifty years, $140.*

and Adolphe Menjou, just to name a few. Cleaverly acts more as a consultant to Poulsen & Skone now, though he is always available if a specially sticky problem arises. He gives them a depth of knowledge and experience available nowhere else in the city.

A Poulsen & Skone custom shoe costs $450–500. The firm takes three months to deliver the first pair, six to eight weeks thereafter. But the shop also carries some wonderful ready-to-wear models. These include its famous suede chukka boot, made since the turn of the century out of heavy reverse calf, $110, its Eton slippers, made of corduroy and leather, $60. Its line of ready-made shoes varies in price from $100–210.

Poulsen & Skone has a two-week sale on its ready-made shoes every January. It sends a representative to the United States for customer orders twice a year. Write directly for information regarding location and dates.

S. FISHER
22/23 BURLINGTON ARCADE
LONDON W1
493–4180
MON.–FRI. 9–5:30, SAT. 9–4:30

S. Fisher is one of a number of lovely men's and women's furnishing shops located in the Burlington Arcade that radiates the look and smell of authentic Old England. Yet there is a specific reason for choosing this shop from among the others. S. Fisher carries the largest selection of John Smedley shirts in the world, and John Smedley makes the finest knit shirts money can buy.

The John Smedley shirt, made of fine-gauge wool or cotton, is the only fully fashioned knit shirt on the market. For many years Allen Solly held that distinction. But when the Solly company left the business, John Smedley bought all the old machinery and continued where Solly left off.

Fisher sells the Smedley long-sleeved wool shirt for $50. The cotton knit shirt is available either in long sleeves at $40 or in short sleeves at $35 for a solid color or $40 for stripes. Fisher also carries a cashmere polo shirt (not by Smedley) for $100.

The finest knit shirt available, by John Smedley of England. These shirts, available in short or long sleeves, are fully fashioned, manufactured on the same machines which once knitted the famous Allen Solly shirt. Cotton lisle, $42.50, all wool, $55. S. Fisher, London.

S. J. PHILLIPS
139 New Bond Street
London W1
629–6261
Mon.–Fri. 10–5

There are undoubtedly more famous jewelers in London, but if you are looking for hard-to-find men's antique jewelry, S. J. Phillips is the place to visit. Installed on New Bond Street since 1860, this Old World shop always has on hand an unusual selection of tie bars, cuff links, studs, and collar pins—many from the 1930's and the turn of the century. Its quality is superb, its service impeccable.

Ask for Mr. DaRosa. If he can't find what you want, he'll make it for you, whether it be simple gold cuff links or a collar pin with a jewel on each end. The shop also offers wonderful initial work, done by the same men who do Asprey's, a more famous and commercial English jeweler.

SULKA
160 New Bond Street
London W1
493–4468
Mon.–Fri. 9–5:30, Sat. 9:30–1

Sulka is a legendary name in men's furnishings, though in recent years this London shop seemed to have forgotten its noble past. In the last two years, fortunately, a new, more ambitious ownership has redone the shop and pointed it back in the direction of its past glories. It is still not the grand Sulka of the 1940's and 1950's but the merchandise is once again of fine quality. The shop carries ties and shirts, but of special interest, as of old, are the elegant pajamas and robes. These are made in beautiful fabrics of cotton, silk and cashmere that are unique to the store. Robes in silk foulards and polka dots are $375; cashmeres, $500; pajamas in cotton poplin are $70, cotton voiles, $90; in silk $120.

SWAINE ADENEY BRIGG & SONS LTD.
185 Piccadilly
London W1
734–4277
Mon.–Fri. 9–5:30, Sat. 9–1

There is nothing more traditionally British than the hunt, and nothing for that spectacularly picturesque sporting event this shop won't furnish—for horse and rider alike: hay nets, hoof oil, veterinary tools, electric clippers, saddles, bridles, whips, horns, riding hats and jodhpurs. Even if you've never been out to the shires, there is much here bound to intrigue and amuse you. Founded more than 100 years ago, Swain Adeney appears much as it did in the late nineteenth century—paneled walls, plush carpeting, the rich smell of leather—which is just the way its customers like it. Indeed worried that some of its regulars (one of whom is Queen Elizabeth herself) might be offended by any radical change in decor, the firm's managers postponed opening its second floor for two years until the same type of mahogany paneling used in the original store could be found for the new stairway.

While Swain Adeney is obviously directed to the sports-minded (in addition to equestrian gear, they carry a full line of fishing, hunting and polo equipment), their most exceptional merchandise is their umbrellas. Naturally every Englishman carries a "brolly." He does so for two reasons: to protect against the inclement weather and for hailing a taxi with aplomb. Each activity is probably done best with the famous Brigg umbrella, the same kind the Queen buys.

Each Brigg umbrella is completely hand-made, each handle is bent "by eye" so each Brigg has its own character. The stick is made of real lancewood with solid nickel fittings. Choosing your Brigg is an exercise of infinite combinations as the umbrella comes in three separate lengths, in silk or in nylon and with a variety of different style, shape and quality handles (or "crooks" as they are called). There is even a racing umbrella with a lizard crook and a 9-karat gold pencil fitted into the neck! Brigg umbrellas start at $50 in nylon, $90 in silk. The handles come in crocodile, lizard, black morocco leather, pigskin or furze. The racing umbrella is $500; the nylon travel umbrella is $100.

The traveling umbrella from Swaine Adeney Brigg & Sons Ltd., London. This Brigg umbrella has been designed to fit perfectly into a suitcase without compromising its durability and protective capacity, $65.

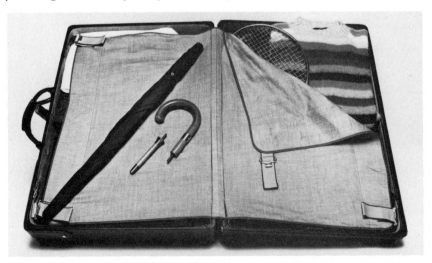

TRICKERS
67 JERMYN STREET
LONDON SW1
930–6395
MON.–FRI. 9–5:30, SAT. 9–12

This ready-to-wear shoe store made its name by selling a sturdily built brogue called "the Tromper." It is by far the largest, clumsiest-looking shoe I have ever seen, but the English have been buying it with enthusiasm for the past 150 years. They use it in the country for walking or hunting, pleased by its comfort and durability.

After Trickers' original customers had bought the Tromper for some time, they began to wonder whether this shop couldn't make in-town styles as well. Soon Trickers was fully into the ready-to-wear shoe business, and today the firm has one of the largest selections in London. Its shoes range in price from $100–200. They are classically English-styled, fully leather-lined and -soled, each manufactured in Trickers' own factory under the strictest standards.

A specialty of Trickers is its offering of slippers, both in leather and velvet. The all leather calf slipper is $50. Plain velvet is $65, and with a gold fox head woven into the toe, $78. Trickers will also make you a pair of velvet slippers with three initials on the toe for $108 or with your own needlepoint pattern for $132.

Until last year when Brooks Brothers joined them, Trickers was the only store in the world to carry an all calf evening pump, $104. Sales take place in January and June.

TURNBULL & ASSER
71-72 JERMYN STREET
LONDON SW1
930–0502
MON.–FRI. 9–5:30, SAT. 9–1

Turnbull & Asser burst onto the fashion scene in the 1960's as the shirt and tie store *par excellence*. While most of London and America were still wearing white or light pastel shirts, Turnbull brought out an entire selection of colored and patterned varieties. It also gave the world the oversized bow tie and the wide 5-inch four-in-hand. There has been no turning back. Today Turnbull & Asser's cotton shirtings in silky poplin and voile come in 830 patterns and stripes, not including solids. Silk crepe de chine shirts, the material woven by their own mill in Lochwinnoch, Scotland, are available in more than thirty colors.

The ties come in a vast selection, each one cut on the true bias and hand-slipped so it never loses its shape. Many are made out of 36-ounce silk, a fabric weight available at few other stores in the world. The stock of bow ties is incomparable, over 3000 on hand at all times.

Curiously not many of the fashion crowd who discovered Turnbull & Asser in the 1960's realized the shop had much of a history. In fact it was founded in 1885 as a maker of hunting gear, then in 1909 it became exclusively a shirtmaker. During the war it designed Winston Churchill's "siren" suits, worn while inspecting London's wartime rubble. The Prime Minister had the shop make dozens of the jumpsuits in different colors, one of which, an emerald green velvet, is preserved under glass in Turnbull's Churchill Room. Noel Coward would buy his silk pajamas and robes from no other store. Charlie Chaplin would order thirty pairs of silk pajamas at a time.

It is always a joy to visit Turnbull—the store is elegantly furnished with richly polished wood details and thick carpets, filled with the magnificent hues of its shirtings, robes and ties. But while its bright-colored furnishings seemed a welcome release in the 1960's, the store's long-collared shirts and bulky napkin-width ties seem overly dramatic today, even a little dated. I would hesitate buying a Turnbull & Asser stock shirt or tie.

On the other hand the robes, which also have oversized collars, are magnificent. They are $115 in cotton, $350 in silk. For real luxury try the ankle-length velvet robe at $625. It will become a family legacy.

Turnbull & Asser silk shirts are $120; its cotton shirts start at $50. The store also has a full selection of cashmere socks in a birds-eye weave for $27.

Each year some time in the middle of January Turnbull & Asser organizes a one-day sale of much of its merchandise. The savings are terrific: silk shirts sell for $40, $100 trousers for $35. But make sure you arrive early. Half of London is liable to be queued up outside waiting for the door to open.

W. BILL LTD.
28 OLD BOND STREET, ROYAL ARCADE
LONDON W1
629–2554
MON.–FRI. 9:30–5:30, SAT. 9:30–1

This store is only eighteen years old, but the Bill family has been in the wool business since the mid-19th century. W. Bill's great grandfather started things off in 1846, opening a factory that manufactured woolen cloths

The multi-striped shetland sweater from W. Bill, Ltd., London. Each sweater is unique, knitted in Scotland with twenty-four different colored stripes, $55.

such as Welsh flannels and tweeds. Today that factory continues to produce, supplying W. Bill Ltd. with exclusive fabrics for its merchandise and exporting the balance outside of England.

W. Bill carries the largest selection of wool tweed ties in the world ($6–14), and the greatest stock of tweed caps in England ($22). These are all made from W. Bill exclusive fabrics, as are the well-cut, English-style tweed jackets at $200. The store also has available an excellent collection of sweaters, including shetlands that are striped with twenty-three separate colors, each sweater unique ($45). It has on the premises a woman who will hand-knit a Fair Isle sweater to order, the only fully hand-knitted Fair Isle sweater available in England. It costs $100.

This store is a must-visit, if only to view what is still so special to England: its tweeds and knits.

WESTAWAY & WESTAWAY
65 Great Russell Street
London WC1
405-4479
Mon.-Fri. 9-5:30, Sat. 9-1

This store has the best knitwear bargains in London. Located across from the British Museum, it carries only top quality goods—the same Fair Isle and shetland sweaters as in the best downtown shops. The company's secret is to buy from the small manufacturers in large quantities. They then sell the merchandise directly out of the boxes. The prices are the lowest in the city, as the mob of eager shoppers inside readily attests. Cashmere sweaters are $85.00; shetlands are $23.00; Fair Isles, $37.50.

Westaway & Westaway can offer you shetland knits in no fewer than sixty colors. Fair Isle sweaters come in an almost equally diverse rainbow. What it doesn't have in stock it will special order.

The ultimate Fair Isle sweater. Specially hand knitted to customers' color and size specifications. Allow six weeks for delivery. A dying breed. W. Bill Ltd., London, $110.

Westaway & Westaway carries only the classic English knits, all made from the finest natural yarns. It staggers its orders so that new things are arriving all the time. There are never any sales. It will ship purchases anywhere in the world.

WILDSMITH & CO.
41 DUKE STREET, ST. JAMES'S
LONDON SW1
930–1623
MON.–FRI. 9–5, SAT. 9:30–12:30

Wildsmith's elegant mail-order brochure states on the cover, "If you already wear our shoes we have a record of your fitting."

There are few stores left in the world where one could expect this kind of record keeping and service for ready-to-wear customers, but Wildsmith raises one's expectations and never disappoints. Located just off Jermyn Street, this firm prides itself not only on the quality of its shoes, but on its service as well. They are a credit to one another, and to the handsome shop itself with its large Persian rug and salesmen dressed in white aprons.

Wildsmith was founded in 1847 and for many years did only custom boot work. Some of its more famous customers in this line included Ray Milland, Cary Grant, David Niven and John Kennedy. Since the War, however, the shop has been producing an excellent collection of ready-to-wear shoes in twenty-eight different styles, from casual suede chukka boots to formal patent leather pumps. There is no finer quality shoe made in London and the styles are excellent. One model I particularly recommend is the calfskin penny loafer in black or brown. Its last is elegantly light, the sole cut close to the shoe's edge.

Wildsmith's ready-to-wear shoes range from $160–300. They are all fully lined. The store has a once a year sale in January.

Milan

MILAN IS the most sophisticated city in Italy. Its fine stores cater to the highly visible fashion set as well as to the retiring millionaires. Both are higher in per capita numbers here than in any other city in the world. Look for fashion merchandise that is made from the finest materials, sewn and finished on a par with the best custom-made goods. Or really splurge and have something made just the way you've always wanted. Italian craftsmanship is still the most exacting in the world and the best in Italy is likely to be found in Milan. Here, as is true throughout Italy, store hours are 9–1 and 3:30–7, Monday through Saturday.

A. CARECENI
VIA FATEBENE FRATELLI, 16
MILAN 20121
66.19.72

Careceni was at one time the most famous name in Italian tailoring. His clientele was an international Who's Who of the world's best-dressed men, and included such luminaries as Douglas Fairbanks and Clark Gable. When Careceni died various relatives immediately opened their own shops, each claiming to be the real descendant or heir to the great Careceni tradition. Today there are almost a dozen Careceni tailors listed in the Milan phone book, including one claiming to be "the real" Careceni.

There is no way to know for certain who the original Careceni might have chosen as his successor, but A. Careceni on the via Fatebene Fratelli is almost the unanimous choice among the *cognoscenti* here as the finest tailor in Milan. He is, in fact, the son of the original Careceni. The store is located above a fabulous bakery shop whose aroma will only increase one's enjoyment in doing business here.

A Careceni suit is designed in the Italian highly shaped tradition. It will fit like an elegant glove and will be finished completely by hand. The choice of materials here is not as extensive as one might assume, but Careceni carries some fabrics unique to the store. One is bound to find something among these.

Suits cost $750–850 and take a month to complete. Three or four fittings are required.

ALBERTINI
VIA GESU, 3
MILAN 20121
70.69.37

You would never guess from seeing this modern storefront that Albertini was begun in 1890. Yet pass through the sales area in front to the workshop in the rear and you are immediately convinced. There men are shaping and sewing leather in the craftsman-like manner that made Italian shoemakers famous.

Albertini can copy a pair of your favorite shoes, design a new look to your own specifications, or suggest an Italian style model from those on hand. A pair of shoes will take two months to complete and will cost $350–375.

BARBAS BIBAS
VIA SANT'ANDREA, 21
MILAN 20121
70.14.26

This store, founded only ten years ago, has quickly achieved a reputation as one of the finest men's fashion shops in the world. Indeed there are members of the international fashion set who fly into Milan for a day just to shop here.

Price is never an object at Barbas. Its sole concerns are quality and styling. That is probably why Giorgio Armani appealed to it from the start. Barbas was the first store in Italy to feature Armani, and the cachet he received for being shown there played no small role in his success.

Barbas is two full floors, a modern elegantly decorated store with sportswear on the ground floor and suits on the second. The merchandise is all of Italian design and manufacture, chosen with impeccable taste. It is probably the most expensive ready-to-wear fashion store in the world, and such quality no longer comes cheaply. Shirts are $80–175, suits $600, and cashmere sweaters $200–300. Look also for the best leather jackets anywhere at $400–800.

BRIGATTI
CORSO VENEZIA, 15
MILAN 20121
70.55.52

Brigatti has often been referred to as the Abercrombie and Fitch of Italy—an apt description if you still remember that once wonderful, now defunct, New York institution. Founded in 1884, this store carries sporting clothes and accessories for almost every active sport, or as its slogan says, *Tutti per tutti gli sport*. If you need proper clothes for hunting with dogs or for riding your ten-speed racer, Brigatti has got them.

The shop itself is panelled in dark wood and is dimly lit, giving it the warm Old World feeling of a country estate, which is the kind of place many of its clientele repair to on the weekends. It is separated into a series of rooms, each dedicated to one or two sports. There is a golf room, a tennis room, a hunting and fishing room, and others. The clothes, unlike much of America's sporting attire, are high-styled and made of beautiful lush materials. The wealthy Italian likes to dress to the teeth, even for a game of doubles!

There are many items to interest the sporting enthusiast, as well as those men just looking for a well-styled jacket or sweater. In this regard particularly I would recommend several of the Brigatti hunting jackets—excellently designed with countless functional pockets and straps ($175–300)—and also the tennis and running warm-up suits in cotton stretch material ($95–185).

CORBELLA
VIA DANTE, 8
MILAN 20121
87.63.79

This prestigious shirtmaking firm is ninety-six years old and now overseen by the third generation of the Corbella family. Though the world has changed around it, Corbella continues to do things in the old manner. Shirts are fitted meticulously to the individual physique, and every stitch, every buttonhole, is sewn by hand.

The store itself is quietly elegant, with its dark rugs and richly polished wood paneling. It houses a vast selection of the finest shirting fabrics available in Europe. Here you will find silks and Egyptian cottons the likes of which are available in few other places.

Such exclusivity and such care is not inexpensive. Shirts are $175 apiece, with a six-shirt minimum order. Figure on a one-month delivery time.

GIORGIO ARMANI
VIA S.ANDREA, 10
MILAN 20121
70.03.85

Giorgio Armani has probably had more impact on the style of men's fashion clothes than any other designer since Pierre Cardin. In the past five years the seriousness that once characterized the high fashion of Europe has been thoroughly undermined by Armani's soft, casual, throwaway chic. He has changed the proportion of lapels, the fit of shoulders, even the shape of the jacket—all with the object of giving formerly austere suits the look and feel of sportswear.

His store in Milan opened in 1979. It has a modern unobtrusive quality—Armani wants the clothes to do the talking. And talk they do. This shop, after all, is Armani's most complete fashion statement. Each season he presents his new collection here and the shop has a different look. The styles are always exciting, the colors marvelous. This is definitely a must to visit. But be aware. These clothes are incredibly expensive, and an Armani jacket of two years ago is already beginning to look dated. Still this is some of Europe's fashion at its best, and the quality of the merchandise is almost without equal in the ready-to-wear market.

Suits are $450–750, shirts $65–140, sweaters $95–200, and trousers $125–195.

LONDON HOUSE
GALLERIA VITTORIO EMANUELE
MILAN 20121
80.79.49

To a visitor this store must seem like an anomaly in the midst of the Milanese shopping district. From the English hunt scenes which decorate the walls to the thoroughly British merchandise its aesthetic seems as far from the Italian mentality as one might imagine. Yet strangely enough the Northern Italians who live and work in Milan have always felt an affinity for England and all things British. Their suits have always been a little less flashy than, say, those of the Romans, and the fabrics they use have a strong English orientation. (The Milanese weather, cold and damp, is not much different from that of London.)

So this beautiful store with its brass fixtures and clubby atmosphere is a Milan institution, and has been for years. Here Italian gentlemen can find the best of the Englishmen's products: Daks trousers and Chester Barrie suits, Aquascutum overcoats and raincoats, John Smedley wool and cotton lisle shirts and Pringle sweaters.

If you're going to visit London there's no reason to shop the London House, though as a store it does have wonderful Old World charm. But if you're not going to London this trip, then by all means come here. It's a home away from home for all serious Anglophiles.

RED AND BLUE
MONTENAPOLEONE, 8
MILAN 20121
79.33.92

This elegant little shop, treasured by all who know it, sells the finest men's furnishings in Italy. Its ability to do so is based on a combination of two factors. To begin with the proprietor, Signor Mazzucchelli, is one of the most knowledgeable men in the furnishings field I've ever met. His taste and style are impeccable. On top of that Mazzucchelli owns his own knitwear factory in the nearby town of Monza. This gives him the ability to produce whatever a customer might desire.

Consequently Red and Blue can make you cotton lisle socks in any length, in any style of ribbing, and in almost any color, including lavender or bright yellow ($11 a pair). It may be the only store in the world with that capability.

It also offers hand-finished cashmere sweaters in fifty colors, including turquoise and pink. These sweaters can be designed in whatever style you like, made from single- or double-ply yarns. They can be ready in less than a month and cost $200 apiece.

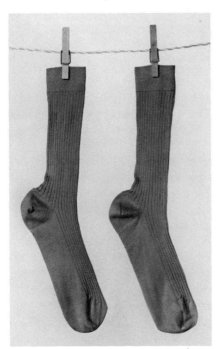

Cotton lisle hosiery from Red and Blue, Milan. This shop is the only one in the world where you can still order custom-made lisle hosiery. Available in any size and length and practically any color, including pink and purple, $11.

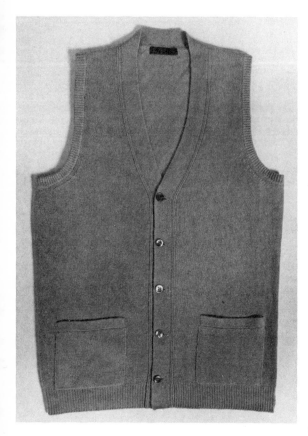

A custom-made cashmere vest from Red and Blue, Milan. This model comes with hand-made buttonholes and silk-lined pockets. It is pink, but customers can select from fifty different shades of yarn and an array of styles, $165.

In stock, Red and Blue carries Europe's best selection of linen hand-kerchiefs with hand-rolled edges. They are available in colors like pink, peach, soft green, and maize ($8–12). Their hand-sewn gloves are also special, though very expensive ($75 and up).

For many Milanese businessmen, Red and Blue is the only shop in which to buy dress shirts. This store has access to exceptional French fabrics made in Ramie. Their cloth is sewn from a special Chinese grass that is grown in India and is softer and finer than any other cotton yarn available. These shirts sell for $135 and come in white and soft pastel colors, yellow and a blue.

Red and Blue will also custom-make cashmere knit shirts ($200), and pajamas with handmade buttonholes in silk ($130) or cotton voile ($85).

I don't know how long Red and Blue can continue to do such fine individualized work in this day and age. But as long as Signor Mazzucchelli is in charge, you can be sure there will be no drop in the standards. The question remains whether enough people will be willing to pay for such personalized attention in the future. I certainly hope so.

TRUZZI
Corso Matteotti, 1
Milan 20121
70.12.08

This shop has been making fine shirts for the Milanese elite since 1890. The seventy-six-year-old owner, Signor Ballini, bought the shop fifty years ago when there were only two seamstresses on hand. Today he employs forty-eight, all of them working on the premises. In fact this shop is so busy that Bellini even finds himself cutting patterns from time to time.

Truzzi fabrics are made from the finest quality cottons and silks, but they are not especially outstanding in terms of design. They tend to be simple colors or patterns. Seeing them, one immediately wonders why so much of Milan's aristocracy should feel the need to go here and spend $150 just to buy a tattersall shirt. The answer has to do with the service and craft. Ballini understands the subtle needs of Milan's older gentlemen, and his shirts are hand-finished with the finesse and quality they have always demanded.

Truzzi requires a minimum three-shirt order.

Paris

PARISIANS HAVE a long history of appreciating goods of the finest quality. French perfume, French wine, French cheese and French food—these are certainly exportable items, but their largest market remains at home. Parisians pride themselves in knowing that what they produce and consume is the best; it is inherent in the French character. Indeed recently the French government has been helping to support and promote just those industries which produce the quality merchandise that is so much a part of France's heritage.

This obsession with quality, as it were, extends to clothes. Paris today continues to have the widest selection of the highest quality goods of any city in the world. From John Lobb shoes to Charvet shirts to Hilditch and Key men's furnishings, there is simply no parallel anywhere. On a Sunday afternoon in Paris it is commonplace to see a businessman take his family out to dine at a two- or three-star restaurant and spend $300 or $400. He feels pleased to do it because he knows he's provided his family with the finest food in the world. Similarly that same man will feel nothing about spending $200 for a custom-made shirt or $1000 for a silk robe. Once again he knows that what he has bought has no equal anywhere.

Of course there is another side to Parisian clothing, a side that caters to the new generation that disdains the old aristocracy's *de rigueur* look of gray slacks and blue blazers. This is the "fashion" crowd that first made American jeans the thing to wear, and has now gone off in other directions. Fashion too, *la mode,* is part of the French heritage, and on the streets of Les Halles or in St. Germain one can always see the latest, wildest, high-styled looks. There is a sense of freedom and excitement in Paris that seems to encourage such experimentation, and one finds things here that only two years later are reaching the general market.

Like the great city it is, Paris promotes the old and the new. One shops here with both nostalgia and adventure.

A. CRISTIANI
2, RUE DE LA PAIX
PARIS 75002
261 12 34
MON.–FRI. 9–12, 2–6:30; SAT. 9–12

This tailoring firm is probably the most meticulous in Paris. One pays for such care. A two-piece wool suit begins at $1250. In cashmere that same suit is $2000.

Founded in 1940 by the present owner's father, A. Cristiani is located in a shop that is every bit as elegant as such prices would lead one to expect. The style is Empire. There are rich mahogany walls with gold trim and moldings, antique furniture and antique rugs. Hung discreetly on the walls are photographs of some of the shop's more famous customers: Gene Kelly, Gary Cooper, Prince Faisal of Saudi Arabia, Vittorio Emmanuel de Savoy, Maurice Chevalier, Louis Jourdan, Mel Ferrer and Marcello Mastroianni.

The Cristiani suit is styled in the traditional Franco-Italian manner, with narrow shoulders, a clean chest and closely fitting waist, and trousers that hang straight. Where it differs significantly is in the detail work. Every piece of the suit is sewn and pieced together by hand. Cristiani's own imported silk is used for the linings with an interior pocket that buttons closed and which has a special compartment for carrying a pen or pencil. All the buttonholes are made by hand, with a different stitch used for those on the sleeve. The lapel buttonhole, rather than slanted, is cut on a horizontal line— a rather peculiar detail which Cristiani insists does a better job of holding the rosettes and decorations which are so much a part of the dress of his esteemed clientele. Finally, in both patterned and striped suits, the collar is attached in such a manner that the stripe or pattern continues without interruption. If a vest is purchased, the material is cut on the bias so that no interruption of pattern or striping occurs here either.

A Cristiani suit requires three fittings and three weeks to complete. For $800 you can have a slightly lesser quality suit, made without silk linings and without the shop's unique pattern matching.

ANAM
15, Avenue Victor Hugo
Paris 75016
501 67 32
Mon.–Sat. 9–12, 2–6

At age sixty-five, Madame Anam is still as intimidating as ever. She says she used to be able to recognize all her customers by their custom-made shoes, but now with so much ready-to-wear being sold, she hardly has a reference point. Even so if Madame Anam does not like your shoes or socks, she will not hesitate to ask you to leave the shop.

That would be unfortunate, for this pocket-sized store has a most wonderful collection of sweaters—cardigans, V-necks, crews and vests, all kept in large plastic bags. They are made from the finest imported wool, most with buttonholes cut and sewn by hand. Anam's specialty is cashmere. This shop carries only the top English quality and its selection is the finest in Paris. Prices range from $140–160. But when you go remember to have your shoes polished first.

AU PETIT MATELOT
27, Avenue de la Grande-Armée
Paris 75016
500 15 51
Tues.–Sat. 10–7, Mon. 2–7

Au Petit Matelot must be one of the oldest continually operating firms in the world. It was founded in 1790 and mentioned by Balzac in his *Lectures about Paris* in 1837. The store's original preoccupation was the outfitting of sailors. But once it changed location from a shop along the Seine to the Avenue de la Grande-Armée, it expanded its market to include almost all outdoor sportsmen. Even so it never stopped selling the famous navy pea coat it invented so long ago.

Today Au Petit Matelot sells some of the most wonderful looking sport clothes in Europe, clothes for horseback riding and horse racing, for yachting, hunting and shooting. Most of these garments are uniquely styled and detailed, made up especially for the store in factories in Italy and France. For their quality level and styling they are hardly expensive.

The store has, to begin with, an excellent selection of knit and wool trousers for walks through forests and mountains. A pair of splendid, extra-thick cavalry twill trousers, the cloth near impenetrable, is $85. Special hunting pants in wool, pleated and with a special velcro opening where boot tops would end, are $80. Down vests for hunting start at $60. A featured hunting vest made of corduroy, down-lined and with detailed pockets to hold ammunition, game, and other paraphernalia, is $85. Other distinctive hunting wear includes a knitted green safari-style jacket, corduroy-trimmed on shoulders and elbows and pile-lined, $135, and an Austrian hunting coat with raglan shooting sleeve, $210.

For riding there are English tweed hacking jackets with leather trim. Smartly cut, they are $200–250.

For sailing there is a blue English flannel blazer, and of course Au Petit Matelot's very own pea coats, made of fine English wool, $175.

This is a store frequented by most of Paris' sporting set. According to some the garments are not what they used to be, the present young owner spending more of his time playing pinball than attending to the shop. But of course the French are always degrading the present in favor of the past. Camus and Sartre, they complain, were never like Balzac. This store is still a joy to visit.

BERLUTI
26, RUE MARBEUF
PARIS 75008
359 51 10
TUES.–SAT. 10–12:30, 2–7:30; MON. 2–7:30

This shoemaking firm, founded in 1895, is now being run by the fourth generation of the Berluti family. Its clients tend to be older gentlemen and businessmen, men looking for finely crafted shoes with a conservative style.

The choice here seems near infinite. Displayed on shelves throughout the shop are over 400 models of shoes, from loafers to hiking boots. Most, however, tend to be slightly heavy looking, though their leathers and hand stitching are as fine as any you might find in Italy.

Berluti makes a famous shoe called the Dorado, which is a business-type oxford that closes with a side buckle. It also makes a shoe unique to the store that shows no stitching on the outside. These shoes, custom-made, take three to four months for delivery and cost $850. In ready-made styles the Berluti shoe is $200–250.

CERRUTI 1881
27, Rue Royale
Paris 75008
265 68 72
Tues.–Sat. 10–6:30, Mon. 2:30–6:30

Cerruti 1881 has perennially the most interesting sportswear in Europe. The designs are consistently fresh, the cloth and knit goods of superior quality. Moreover if one had to buy a ready-to-wear suit in Paris, one could do no better than to shop here. The fabrics are from the Cerruti mill, one of the finest in the world, and the cut is superb for Franco-Italian classic clothes. Small wonder then that its clientele reads like a Who's Who in the world of fashion and celebrity, people like Johnny Halliday, Margaux Hemingway, Michael York, Mick Jagger, Paloma and Claude Picasso, Rod Stewart, Jean Claude Killy, Louis Malle, Gene Wilder and Jean Amadou.

Cerruti itself is a large manufacturing company employing over 2000 people. Founded in 1881 as a weaving concern, it now maintains several factories in Italy which weave wool materials and manufacture ready-to-wear clothing and one factory in Scotland which does knitwear, particularly in cashmere.

Cerruti 1881 was opened in Paris in 1967. The shop has a completely contemporary look designed by the Italian architect Magistretti. It is a provocative mixture of glistening black-and-white walls and mirrors, and is completely carpeted and divided into a series of small rooms, one leading to the next. Inside these you will find stylish shirts, sweaters, trousers and suits. Naturally, as this is a "fashion" store, the merchandise is constantly changing. But one can count on quality here as well as design that will not lose its impact.

Sweaters range in price from $60–150; odd trousers in wool gabardine or corduroy $80–150; shirts in pima cotton $40–80; suits $400–550, depending on material.

Sales take place in January and July.

CHARVET
8, Place Vendome
Paris 75001
260 30 70
Tues.–Sat. 10–6:30; Mon. 2–6:30

For most of the 1920's and 1930's five shops were universally accorded the designation as the finest men's furnishing stores in the world—Poirier,

Seelio, Seymour, Bouvin, and Charvet. Today only Charvet remains. Founded in 1850, it continues to turn out the highest quality shirts, pajamas, robes, socks, suits, ties and underwear—everything for a man's wardrobe except shoes and hats. Not long ago the French government, in appreciation of Charvet's unique image, arranged a special exhibition at the Louvre of its antique shirts, made at the turn of the century. This exhibition, an example of French workmanship and design at its best, is now permanently housed in a shop on the Rue Matignon, a street of art galleries, and paid for by a grant from the French government.

Up until fifteen years ago, Charvet was a family business that operated in much the same manner as it had when the founder, the shirtmaker Edouard Charvet, was alive. Very little was displayed; a customer was shown only what he requested. In most cases this was something fairly conservative. Most shirts sold were white, blue, cream or a subtle stripe.

After Mr. Colban bought the store, things began to change. It started when Baron Rothschild came into the store and asked to see some shirt

The finest dress shirt in the world by Charvet, Paris. Notice in particular the placing of the sleeve placket button, made from thick mother-of-pearl. Collar has been made with no excess tie space, $100.

swatches. One of these happened to be pink. Questioned about it, Colban, following previous Charvet custom, responded that pink was not for him. To which Rothschild retorted, "If it's not for me, who is it for?"

Some time later Nelson Rockefeller requested some shirt swatches be sent to New York. Colban, much to the horror of the Charvet workers, decided to send along with the blues, whites and creams some bold stripes and unusual colors. Of course the order came back with the more exciting shirt fabrics chosen.

From that point on Colban changed the point-of-view of Charvet as well as its role with the customer. Now when you walk into this Regency-style store in Paris' most graceful square, the Place Vendome, you find fabrics piled high on old mahogany tables, or elegantly strewn about the shop. Colban is trying to inspire the customer, though if he chooses something that doesn't quite suit him, Colban has no compunction about telling him so.

Yet Colban is more than just a very fine retailer. He is a design experimenter constantly trying out new ideas at a quality level unavailable elsewhere in Europe. He owns his own weaving mill so he can design his own patterns for shirtings and ties. And because so many of Europe's top designers and couturiers get their shirts made at Charvet, Colban is able to learn what is happening on the contemporary scene.

Presently Colban says, "Style is more important than quality for most people. I want to give both." He keeps on hand a wide variety of the finest made poplins, linens and silks in sufficient quantity so that they are always available. Indeed, the Japanese have recently been buying silk from him, as the top quality is in short supply there.

A Charvet shirt, though not sewn on the premises, is made in a factory three hours away. Each shirt, whether custom or ready-to-wear, is made by one woman who does everything except sew the buttonholes and iron. The buttons are made of a thick mother-of-pearl that always makes one feel very rich.

Charvet ties are made from hand-loomed silk. They are cut at the factory, then taken home to be sewn by one of the workers.

The robes are made by the same tailors who make the suits and overcoats. This experience gives these tailors a special expertise, particularly in the making of heavy woolen robes which are constructed very much like overcoats. The detail work is simply extraordinary.

Prices at Charvet are as expensive as one might expect. Custom shirts are $105–160, ready-to-wear $75–105. Custom wool robes are $215–400, ready-to-wear $175–350. Custom suits are $1200, adapted measure $750. Ties are $30–50. Yet in a world where machines are fast replacing human labor and there is no one to hand down the knowledge and experience of old school craftsmanship, Charvet stands alone, still possessing the spirit and ability to create anything a client can dream of, and sometimes more.

CIFONELLI
31, RUE MARBEUF
PARIS 75008
723 38 84
MON.–FRI. 9–12:30, 2–6, SAT. 9–12:30

This tailor is considered by many to be the finest in Paris. Cifonelli caters to the city's aristocracy as well as to a very select group of internationals. Indeed, having a suit made here is almost like joining a kind of elite club with dues set accordingly. A two-piece wool suit starts at the unbelievable price of $1800.

Founded in 1931 by Arturo Cifonelli, the firm is now run by Arturo's son, Adriano, who took over after his father's death in 1972. Suits and overcoats continue to be made with the same impeccable style and meticulous quality that first brought Cifonelli to the notice of Paris' fine dressers. All work is completed by hand and only pure silk linings are used.

What distinguishes a Cifonelli suit is the treatment given the shoulders. The sleeve head is fitted with great precision and rounded in a way that makes it clear it has not been set in by machine. The armhole is cut high, affording a man a longer look as well as a great freedom of movement. The jacket stays put on the shoulder no matter how much the arms move.

Cifonelli is a true artisan. Entering the second-floor shop via a grand marble stairway, then through a heavy mahogany door, one is prepared to find some of the finest clothes money can buy. Cifonelli does not disappoint.

DELAUNAY
159, BOULEVARD ST. GERMAIN
PARIS 75006
548 37 80
MON.–SAT. 9:30–7:30

Delaunay is actually one of four special stores owned by Michel Barnes. I have selected it in particular because Barnes is usually here, and he is the man with the special eye. Yet all four shops, modern affairs in light wood, operate in similar fashion and one would do well visiting any of them. The others are:

Barnes, 61, Avenue Victor Hugo, 500 98 10
Charles Bosquet, 13, Avenue Marbeuf, 225 25 51
Harrison, 130, Rue de la Pompe, 727 96 62.

Barnes has fabulous personal style and he adores the suit. His concept is to give men the opportunity to have suits made that have a little more detail and choice of styling than normal off-the-rack suits and yet are not much more expensive. He does this with made-to-measure suits that are sewn by machine and which are not cut on individual patterns but based on models he has already designed. Four styles are available to customers, three classic British and European cuts and a Brooks Brothers–type model with soft fused fronts and tailor-made lapels.

Barnes has a wide selection of English and Italian fabrics: wools for winter, some wash-and-wears and cottons for summer.

A suit requires two to three fittings and is ready in fifteen days. The price is $300–450, depending upon the fabric. For $20 additional you can have hand-made buttonholes. Cashmere sportjackets are $300.

Barnes also carries some tasteful British-American styled furnishings. Sales on this merchandise and on some of the ready-made suits take place in June and January.

GLOBE
12, RUE PIERRE LESCOT
PARIS 75001
508 98 53
MON.–SAT. 10:30–7

When Globe opened in 1974 it was the talk of the Paris fashion crowd. To begin with there was the store itself, a true high-tech inception that traded exposed heating pipes for the traditional slick glass and chrome, a concept which many say later influenced the design of the Pompidou Museum. Next came the clothes. Peter Fournier, a real sartorial intellectual, wanted none of the typical Franco-Italian avant-garde designs. Instead in this severely modern setting he chose to show classics from all over the world. He sold Bass Weejun loafers next to French hospital workers' clothes. He also had American jeans, English mesh riding gloves, and caricature high-tech wraparound glasses. In addition he had antique clothing! The effect was profound. Many people did not understand what he was doing and they were concerned that he was crazy. But in many respects Globe was the most important contemporary store to be founded in the past decade. Fournier was showing fashion that was classic. In other words, here was clothing, he said, to be contemporary in. And yet one didn't have to worry that tomorrow that clothing would no longer be in style.

Globe continues today in this manner. The stock changes periodically but Fournier is always hunting for items that are ageless. The prices are moderate. The hospital workers' clothes, for example, are $10. White bucks are $50.

HEMISPHERES
22, Avenue de la Grande Armée
Paris 75017
755 61 86
Mon.–Sat. 10:30–7

This store is actually more than forty years old but it's only in the last two years that Paris' fashion crowd has been compelled to take notice of it. The explanation for this sudden change in fortunes is not terribly complicated. The management of the store changed hands in 1978 and none other than Peter Fournier, the provocative founder of Globe, took over.

Fournier has continued the revolution he started at Globe, selling classics from all over the world but presenting them in the eclectic mix that is today's most important fashion statement. A typical mannequin might be wearing madras pants, cowboy boots and a quilted Western jacket, a brilliant conception. Hemispheres carries considerably more merchandise than Globe does and there is no limit on their price or quality.

John Smedley cotton lisle shirts from England, the finest in the world, are $40. Fabulous American nylon parkas with Western-style leather yokes are $100–125.

Hemispheres carries a large selection of madras trousers, Levi's 501 jeans, Rocky Mountain ski parkas, and outrageous multi-colored sweaters. Its beautiful shoes are from England; they are classically British in style and cost $85–135.

Hemispheres is the most exciting contemporary store in Paris and perhaps all of Europe. It is the brainchild of Peter Fournier, and he is an original.

HILDITCH AND KEY
252, Rue de Rivoli
Paris 75001
260 36 09
Mon.–Sat. 9–6:30

Hilditch and Key is the most expensive men's furnishing firm in the world . Since 1913 this quietly elegant two-story shop has been servicing the French upper class (as well as a star-studded array of international visitors) in

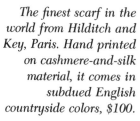

The finest scarf in the world from Hilditch and Key, Paris. Hand printed on cashmere-and-silk material, it comes in subdued English countryside colors, $100.

a manner that permits no compromise. If Hilditch and Key carries a garment its fabric will be the finest available; its manufacture and detailing will be done in ultimate taste and style.

For example its cashmere cardigan sweater costs $400. The sweater is made from England's finest cashmere and pieced together by hand. The buttonholes are hand-made, the pockets are trimmed by hand and they are even lined in silk. It is simply the best. An alpaca V-neck sweater at $200 has no equal anywhere in the world.

Hilditch and Key makes its own ties and scarves and these are also a specialty. The style of the ties is primarily English. They come in beautiful silk foulards and checks in 3-inch widths as well as in cashmere and wool ($35-60).

The Hilditch and Key scarf is a cashmere and silk combination. In English country colors it is $85-120.

Because of its English orientation, one would expect Hilditch and Key to carry umbrellas. Naturally it does, and only the finest, the Brigg umbrella, $50-150. It also carries the best quality white hand-rolled linen handkerchiefs in Paris, the largest collection of patterned hosiery, and perhaps the most beautiful silk foulard and paisley robes in the world. These are made from a heavy silk twill and start at $1000.

Of course no traditional men's furnishings shop (and Hilditch and Key is nothing if not traditional) would be complete without its shirt department. Hilditch and Key makes all its own shirts on the premises and its custom shirt may well be the finest available. The shoulders are put in by hand, as is the collar. The buttonholes are sewn by hand. All shirts are made out of the finest cotton fabrics and start at $125.

Hilditch and Key's aim is to produce the best merchandise available anywhere in the world and in this it rarely fails. If you have money, this is the place to go. Whatever you spend, it will not be wasted.

LANVIN
15, Rue de Faubourg Saint-Honoré
Paris 75008
265 14 40
Mon.–Sat. 9:30–1, 2–6:30

Lanvin is one of the few big name designer shops still turning out credibly styled, quality merchandise for men. Madame Lanvin believed in elegance, and this belief continues to govern the workings of the store, itself one of the most elegant in Paris. Designed in 1926 by Rateau, the store remains unchanged from the day it opened, its special meurisier wood as brightly polished as ever. Placed about the store are marvelous Art Deco figurines, beautiful velvet chairs, and display cases with handsome brass appointments—elegance with a purely French character.

Lanvin still carries the largest selection of solid and printed silk shirts in Paris. These are completely finished by hand, including the shoulder seams and buttonholes, by workmen on the premises. They sell for $140–185.

Its collection of French printed ties, made from its own specially patterned silk, is unrivaled by any store in the world. Lanvin sells 18,000 a year, each costing $50–60. At any one time the store has 3000–4000 on hand. Its scarves, made from the same tie silk, are also sewn and stitched by hand.

Hose is another Lanvin specialty. Look for the interesting collections of cotton lisle socks with hand-embroidered clocks or motifs. In short and garter length, these sell for $8–12 a pair. They come, unfortunately, in no pastel colors but in blacks, grays and burgundy.

Finally one should not overlook the Lanvin robes. The ready-to-wear robes are spectacular, sewn by the same workmen and in the same manner as their custom robes. In beautiful solid silks in foulard or patterns, they are $400; in cashmere, $800.

This is a store in the grand French tradition. It is nice to know the tradition lives on.

JOHN LOBB
47, FAUBOURG SAINT-HONORÉ
PARIS 75008
265 24 45
MON.–SAT. 9:30–1, 2:15–6:30

The people at Lobb like to tell two stories about this world-renowned shoemaker. The first concerns Basil Zaharoff, the famous allied agent and armament provider of World War I. Zaharoff loved Lobb shoes and kept dozens of pairs in his Paris house. When his death became imminent he asked Lobb to make him a pair with a completely new last. He knew he would die before he could ever wear them, but he loved Lobb shoes so much he just wanted to know they were in the works.

The second story concerns an Arabian prince who visited Lobb one day and requested it make him the most expensive shoes in the world. Three months later Lobb presented the prince with a pair of $7000 crocodile-skin boots.

These stories illustrate two interesting points about Lobb. First, Lobb customers tend to establish lifelong relationships with the firm; they are almost fanatic about their shoes. Second, there is almost no shoemaking demand Lobb cannot fulfill.

The Paris Lobb is still owned by the British family of John Lobb, but the shoes and boots they produce are infinitely superior to those of their English brethren. Located on the second floor of Hermes, in my mind the most beautiful store in the world, Paris Lobb is privileged to employ seventeen workmen whose average age is sixty. These are craftsmen of the old school, originally apprenticed by Lobb and now true masters of their field. They can make anything in shoewear from silk evening pumps to old-fashioned button shoes, from crocodile loafers to musketeer hip-height riding boots.

Prices at Lobb begin at $800 for a pair of shoes, though often the cost is closer to $1000. Three months are required to make the first pair of shoes, six weeks thereafter.

The Lobb product is without question one of the finest in the world.

MARCEL LASSANCE
17, Rue du Vieux Colombier
Paris 75006
548 29 28

66, Champs Elysées
Paris 75008
723 30 96
Mon.–Sat. 10–7

This store offers consistently fine sportswear for men. Marcel Lassance, the owner, is a talented designer whose taste fluctuates somewhere between American Brooks Brothers and French St. Tropez. He sells "fashion," but at a high level of quality and style. Like Cerruti, this is a store whose merchandise manages to combine classic sophistication with contemporary energy. This is particularly true of the sweaters and shirts which are always special.

Shirts range in price from $50–75, sweaters from $75–125. Marcel Lassance also carries interesting trousers, $60–100, sportjackets, $75–125 and English shoes, $85–125.

MASSARO
2, Rue de la Paix
Paris 75002
261 00 29
Mon.–Fri. 9–1, 2–6:30, Sat. 9–1

This firm has been making custom-made shoes in Paris for seventy years; first only shoes for women, then in the past ten years, men's shoes. More than 200 models in different lasts and leathers are displayed on shelves about this three-room atelier overlooking the venerable Rue de la Paix. The shoes have a slightly younger, lighter look than those found at Lobb, Paris' grand shoemaker. This Massaro attributes to his initial education in the making of women's shoes. The styles have an elegant but distinctly Franco-Italian look.

A pair of Massaro shoes, found on the feet of some of Paris' most illustrious personalities, start at $550. They require six to eight weeks to finish.

MEXICO-LINDO
19, RUE DES CANETTES
PARIS 75006
326 43 55
MON.–SAT. 10–1, 2–7:20, MON. OPEN LATE

This wonderful boutique sells Western gear with all the excesses of a Spanish down-on-the-border mentality. And it is no Johnny-come-lately in the drugstore cowboy field. For twenty-two years it has been a Paris fashion standby, its tiny space crammed full of colorful boots, shirts and belts. Today much of its merchandise is readily available to Americans, but one can occasionally find a one-of-a-kind belt buckle or multi-tone boot made in Mexico especially for this shop.

Whatever one buys here, the quality is always first rate; the styles and the window designs are invariably outrageous.

Boots sell for $100–300, belt buckles for $25–160.

PAUL PORTES
194, RUE DE RIVOLI
PARIS 75001
260 55 34
MON.–FRI. 9–6

Small purchases at Paul Portes are often given to customers in burlap bags that are designed to look like those used to keep money in by the Bank of France. This seems entirely appropriate given the price of the merchandise here. Two-piece custom-made suits, for example, begin at $1200, shirts at $115.

Paul Portes carries everything for a man except shoes, hats and gloves. Its prices are steep though there is no denying the quality of the material and the expertise that go into the construction of each of its articles. In 1962 Jacques Portes, present owner and son of the founder, was given the Gold Scissors Award, the highest honor bestowed by Italy's tailoring association. Today Portes is the president of Paris' Association of Grand Tailors.

A Portes suit takes three weeks and three fittings to complete. It will be sewn completely by hand by workmen who have usually begun their careers right in this shop. Its style is classically Franco-Italian, or as Portes says, "modern but not eccentric." And while waiting for a fitting one will have the opportunity to take in one of the most breathtaking views in Paris—a look over the gardens of the Tuileries and the Louvre.

Portes makes its own ties by hand out of silk that is designed specially for the store, $40. It also sells a noteworthy pair of hose made from 65 percent cashmere, 15 percent silk and 20 percent nylon, $15.

RHODES & BROUSSE
14, RUE DE CASTIGLIONE
PARIS 75001
OPERA 86 27
MON.–SAT. 9–1, 2–6:30

This fine Parisian chemisier is fifty-five years old and it has been making its shirts in the same way for the past forty years. This means a customer can count on a completely hand-finished garment, including the buttonholes, as well as Rhodes & Brousse's two unique collar details. The collar on each of their shirts is left "open," or unlined underneath the back so that it folds correctly and without difficulty after washing and ironing. Furthermore a band is placed under each collar point through which the tie can be threaded so that it is held firmly in place.

A custom shirt takes three to four weeks to finish and costs $110. Rhodes & Brousse has a small but excellent selection of fine Egyptian cotton materials available for viewing in both bolts and swatches. It will make pajamas from these choice fabrics, $115–150, or robes from silk foulard, wool or a wool-cashmere mixture, $300–550.

UPLA
17, RUE DES HALLES
PARIS 75001
261 49 96
MON.–SAT. 10:30–7:30

Upla is one of Paris' fine young sportswear shops, one of a number in recent years that has become fascinated with the casual looks from America and England. For an American, much of this merchandise is available at home. But here in Paris, in this chic contemporary store, it has a somewhat different look. One can really begin to appreciate how wonderful most of these simple garments are.

Upla carries Smith overalls, Fruit of the Loom T-shirts, Alden shoes (the company that manufactures Brooks Brothers classic shoes), and Arrow sportshirts. In addition, it always has a good selection of outerwear like Mac-Gregor drizzler jackets. The clothing is simple and stylish.

Curiously it took the French to teach Americans about the natural elegance of their jeans. Now they may be doing the same thing with American sportswear.

Rome

THE ROMAN man has always shown an intense interest in the shape and style of the clothes he wears. Such a preoccupation would, one assumes, insure a wealth of fine clothing shops and thus a grand opportunity for the foreign visitor looking to refurbish his wardrobe. Indeed, for many years it did. Yet recently Rome seems to have lost some of its attractiveness as a center for the buying of men's clothes.

There is no denying that one can still get things made extremely well here. Italian craftsmanship is some of the finest in the world. Custom suits and shirts are sewn completely by hand; shoes are small pieces of art. But with the country's rampant inflation of the past few years, prices for custom-made clothes have skyrocketed, surpassing many other European and American markets. In addition the style of dress has changed. Instead of selecting the severely cut Italian silhouette, young people seem to be choosing looser, more casual clothes, in the vein of traditional British-American styling. Such clothing is simply not available in Rome.

Things could change here in the next few years though that seems unlikely. In the meantime one thinks nostalgically of what Rome used to be, and shops with less excitement and more caution. Generally, store hours in Italy are 9–1 and 3:30–7, Monday through Saturday.

ANGELO
VIA BISOLATI, 36
ROME
481 796 464 092

Angelo is one of the largest and best known tailoring firms in Rome. Employing 45 sewers and 3 cutters, it produces 1700 custom-made suits a year. The reason for its success is no doubt due to Angelo himself, a charming, ego-less man who puts his customers at ease and immediately removes any anxiety in ordering a suit. A former manager of the famous Brioni's, Angelo Vitucci is probably the easiest tailor to work with for a newcomer to the custom field. Small wonder that he has a strong following in America.

Angelo's workers are nearly all older men, the last of a breed of cutters and sewers who insist on the accuracy and perfection of each aspect of their craft. They work patiently in the back of the first floor where the fitting rooms are situated. Upstairs is the fabric showroom. Angelo stocks a broad selection of suitings from the finest houses in Italy, including some unusual silks and cashmeres. An Angelo suit, styled and shaped in the classic Italian manner, will cost $750. It generally needs three weeks to be completed. Even considering the fine quality of material and workmanship involved that is quite a substantial price. But as Angelo says, "to make a custom-made suit today you do it for love, not money."

Angelo also has on hand a selection of ready-made suits in beautiful English and Italian fabrics, $400–450.

ANGELO LITRICO
Via Sicilia, 51
Rome
475-4313

Litrico is the most prominent men's tailor in Rome. You might think otherwise when you first enter his shop. The carpets are a bit frayed and the whole place has a slightly run-down quality. But when you see the photographs on the wall of the customers Litrico has clothed, you recognize at once how inaccurate first impressions can be. Litrico even makes the Pope's vestments.

A Litrico suit is styled in the traditional Italian manner with absolutely clean, body-hugging lines. Its workmanship is superb, every stitch, every buttonhole sewn by hand. It is, not incidentally, the most expensive suit in Italy: $1500 for a two-piece worsted, single- or double-breasted. Such a price seems totally unrealistic, and yet Litrico has more customers than he can handle, many of whom would probably give up buying suits if they were forced to go elsewhere. Who can ever make sense of what goes on in Rome?

ARTURO FALASCA
Via Fontanella di Borghese, 71
Rome
689 765

Falasca is one of Rome's unheralded wonders. In business in his tiny shop since 1938, he makes as fine a suit as can be found anywhere in Italy. The cost: $325–375.

Falasca carries Cerruti as well as fine English fabrics and he will hand-make every inch of your suit himself. He is a superb craftsman. His one drawback for Americans is his inability to speak English. Yet with a dictionary and a little sign language one can do just fine. Or better yet bring along a friend who speaks Italian.

A suit normally takes ten days and three fittings to complete but if you are pressed for time Falasca can sometimes do it in four days. He is a lovely man and his suits may well be the best buy in Rome.

BATTISTONI
Via Condotti, 57-61A
Rome
67 86 241

Battistoni has for many years been considered the finest shirtmaker in Rome, if not all of Italy. Its customers have included the Duke of Windsor, Gianni Agnelli, and the royal families of Italy, the Netherlands and Greece.

Founded in 1945, the store is now run by Gianni Battistoni, the son of the original owner. To get there one must pass under an archway of the Via Condotti, then through a courtyard and another archway which shelters a beautiful tiny square decorated with flowers. At the rear of the square is the Battistoni shop with its handsome blue and white awnings. Inside there is a series of small rooms, each appointed with crystal chandeliers, antique tables and gold-framed paintings. From within hardly a sound can be heard of the bustle of Rome.

Each Battistoni shirt is made completely by hand. It comes with special mother-of-pearl buttons and takes one fitting and three weeks to complete. Sea Island voiles, of which there is a dazzling collection, cost $85–95. A three-shirt minimum order is required.

BISES
Via del Gesu, 93
Rome
67 80 941

Bises is a fabric store with the most extraordinary collection of piece goods in the world. Housed in a four-story palazzo complete with centuries-old frescos, it offers almost every kind of fabric you could possibly imagine—silks, knitted cottons and wools—even terry cloths and sheeting fabrics. Indeed if you can't find the cloth you're looking for here, it probably wasn't made that season.

Bises is the exclusive agent in Italy for Viyella, that comfortable English cloth of brushed cotton and wool. Often it will have the newest Viyella shirt range in the store before you can even see it in London. The store also carries the overruns of material of the Italian design houses, fabrics from Valentino, Armani and Missoni.

The first floor of Bises carries only shirtings, for both men and women. Fine cotton is $7–10 a yard. Approximately 2½ yards of material is needed to make a shirt.

The second and third floors have wool suitings ($20–50 a yard), corduroys, plain and printed velvets ($3.50–15.00 a yard).

The top floor is for the Viyella ($6 a yard), special silks ($30 a yard) and knitted fabrics ($12–30 a yard). It is crowned with a ceiling that must be 30 feet high and patterned with frescoes. Seeing those lovely fabrics juxtaposed with the historic art of the building is an experience not to be missed.

This store would probably seem an anomaly in the United States. But here in Rome where so much is custom-made it is an extravagant necessity.

CAMOMILLA
Piazza di Spagna, 84-85
Rome
67 93 551

Camomilla is *the* "hot" store on the Continent. If you want something special for disco dressing this is the place to visit. You will not be alone. Everyone young and hip passing through Rome seems to check in here, people like the Rolling Stones.

Camomilla is primarily for women, but the owner, Alan Journo, is constantly on the lookout for outrageous things for men. He flies to Paris,

London and the States. When he returns he is never empty-handed. Even if he hasn't managed to find just the clothes he wanted, he brings back the greatest music months before it becomes popular in the States. You can hear it playing all day long—from the moment Camomilla opens for business each morning until it closes and everyone, Journo included, leaves for dinner and the discos.

The store looks like some kind of mad bazaar, two floors of clothes and unusual articles strewn about in an appearance of complete disorder. For men this is really an item store. There's no telling what you might find on a given day: an extraordinary leather jacket, a secondhand shirt or an authentic, lightweight English flying suit ($75).

But even if you're not in the mood to buy, it's great fun to visit Camomilla. Go there if only to soak up the music and the excitement and the bright colors of beautifully dressed bodies glittering like the stars at a Hollywood opening.

CARLO PALAZZI
VIA BORGOGNONA, 7B-7C
ROME
679 1508

This shop opened in 1965 and almost from the start it garnered a rich and influential clientele. Palazzi appreciated the classics but he also thought clothing should be exciting for men. So he designed for his shop the first man's contemporary full-length fur coat. Later he did the first loose, oversized cloth coat. He also introduced the trouser and matching shirt jacket and the first deep-toned shirts—browns, blues, grays—that became the height of style in the late 1960's.

Today he continues in these two directions, producing updated Italian classics and fashion innovations. His clientele remains the rich and famous—Hassan II, King of Morocco, Rock Hudson and Marlon Brando—as well as numerous French and Italian film directors who have used him to design the wardrobes for their films. His most famous to date: *La Cage aux Folles*.

The shop itself is a rebuilt seventeenth-century palazzo. Its interior has been given an update, a modern geometric look with carpeting and antiques to soften and highlight the simplicity of the design. The ground floor displays shoes and ties, while the upstairs is divided into several smaller areas for the viewing and fitting of shirts, suits and sportswear.

But Palazzi's forte is really sportswear. The shop always carries excellent fine-gauge knit sweaters ($85–175), some great knit shirts ($35–85) and marvelous leather jackets ($225–375).

Palazzi is not a copyist but an artist who directs all his creative energy on the merchandise of his shop. This makes it an exciting place to visit, a store where one can find quality and creativity combined in wholly original ways. If the merchandise is expensive it is only because it is so finely produced and in quantities that resemble less a retail store than a couturier house.

GALTRUCCO
Via del Tritone, 23
Rome
67 89 022

Like Bises, Galtrucco is a fabric store directed at the individual man having clothes custom-made. Where Bises's specialty is sportswear and shirting fabrics, Galtrucco's is suitings. It buys the best quality English and Italian worsteds and woolens direct from the mills. If you appreciate fine wool gabardine—and Italy makes the best—this is the place to buy it. Cerruti and Zegna, the top-of-the-line, are $30–50 a yard. They are stocked all year round in an array of classic suiting colors.

Galtrucco sells the finest worsted and flannels. In addition it carries a large selection of dupioni silks and linens and some unusual 100 percent cotton suitings. These fabrics range in price from $15 a yard to $60 for cashmere. A two-piece suit requires 3¼ yards of material if the width is 60 inches or 150 centimeters.

GATTO
Via Salandra, 34
Rome
474 1450

Gatto is a unique Roman institution. He does no advertising and his "shop" is actually a small apartment in a rather modest building. Yet for years he has been making shoes for the finest Roman families, former princes and kings, actors, actresses and industrialists.

How does he manage? Simple. He makes a completely hand-crafted shoe with meticulous detailing and superb styling. The prices, starting at $225, are well below his closest competitors.

Before you rush off to Gatto, however, telephone first. His "shop" is run like a private home, and sometimes he's just not there. Shoes take approximately two months to complete.

MICOCCI
LARGO FONTANELLA DI BORGHESE, 78
ROME
678 0587

This is hardly the kind of shop that attracts celebrities, but Micocci makes excellent shirts at prices considerably less expensive than its more famous competitors. Begun in 1932 by Signor Micocci's mother, the shop now has 4 women working in the back who do beautiful cutting and handwork on shirts, robes and pajamas.

The store is rather small but nevertheless carries an excellent selection of fabrics in cotton voiles ($55–60), Viyella ($55–60) and silk ($80). The silks are particularly interesting since many of them are old patterns no longer being manufactured. Micocci will make shirts in a week or, if you call in advance, in three days.

The shop also does great silk robes, a good buy at $110, and cotton pajamas for $85.

TESTA
VIA BORGOGNONA, 13
ROME
679 6174
VIA FRATTINA, 104-105-106
ROME
679 1294

These elegant shops with their sepia-toned walls, their marble, glass and chrome furnishings carry the most interesting sportswear in Rome. The clothes are high-styled and fashioned but never so exotic as to be eccentric.

Testa is an imaginative and creative stylist and almost all the merchandise the store sells he has designed himself. The upstairs of his stores are devoted exclusively to his ready-to-wear suits and outerwear. These are made from fine Italian fabrics and cut less severely than the Italian norm. In wool worsteds the suits are $290–310. The overcoats, always classically styled, are $275–350.

Downstairs are the shirts and sweaters. The sleek-fitting patterned sweaters are particularly creative ($50–95), as are Testa's knit shirts ($40–70).

Testa has yet to try wholesaling his merchandise in any large way to stores outside of Italy but it wouldn't surprise me if that comes soon. His clothes are always interesting and in most cases their particular styles are unavailable anywhere else.

Vienna

THIS HIGHLY stylized Old World city is certainly not a place one rushes to for the purchase of men's clothing. Its charms lie elsewhere. The general man's look is stodgy, a boring Germanic style. And yet if your travels happen to take you here, and if you have the time and interest, there are some shops worth browsing in.

Of special interest is the local sport and outerwear, made to last a lifetime and with a functional styling that will not soon date it. There are touches of menswear elegance to be found here as well. But for American dollars this elegance often comes at a dear price.

GEORG MATERNA
MAHLERSTRASSE 5
VIENNA, 1
524 165
MON.–FRI. 8–12:30, 2–6, SAT. 11–12

Founded in 1927 to produce the finest shoes and boots in Austria, Georg Materna is still around to insure this ambition survives in a world of steadily decreasing values. His shoes are truly some of the most beautiful in the world, elegantly styled and superbly crafted.

The shop itself is a new one. Materna has been there only seven years. But to watch his workmen turning skins of the most supple leather into a stylish array of shoes and boots is to feel the clock has been turned back sixty years. Such dedication and craft is the true legacy from that period when Vienna was at the height of its social and cultural prominence.

The style of Materna shoes is typically Anglo-European. The lasts are delicately turned and every stitch is sewn by hand. Yet even with such care the price of a pair of shoes is hardly exorbitant by today's standards. Calf leather shoes start at $340. They take eight to ten weeks to finish.

Materna also has on hand ten styles of ready-to-wear shoes. These start at $275 a pair. Each is made completely by hand and without exaggeration they are the most attractive ready-to-wear shoes I have ever seen.

The last time I visited Materna a young man of seventeen was being fitted for a pair of country-style brogues. I asked him whether $350 wasn't a lot of money to spend on shoes for someone his age. He answered, "Not if my foot doesn't grow. These shoes will last as long as I live." It was a surprise, of course, to find a teenager with such a long-range view of things. And as I looked at his shoes I couldn't help but agree that indeed his investment was a sound one.

KNIZE
GRABEN 13
VIENNA, 1
522 119
MON.–FRI. 9–6, SAT. 9–12:30

This century-old firm has achieved landmark status in Vienna not only for the quality of its suits and accessories, but also for its premises. Completed in 1910 by the distinguished Austrian architect, Adolph Loos, this shop remains a stunning example of the *Yugenstile,* a beautifully balanced construction of glass, mirror and blond inlaid woods.

Knize's "landmark" status means this building cannot be altered without government permission. This suits Tourner Niedersuss, the present director, just fine. He is a traditionalist by nature having learned his tailoring trade as a young man right in this shop. He insists that Knize suits be made today as they were fifty years ago when Adolphe Menjou and Maurice Chevalier shopped here.

Such insistence translates into a lot of man-hours, and at current Austrian wage levels Knize suits are no longer bargains. A custom-made two-piece suit presently costs $1150. For that price, however, you will receive a superbly crafted, natural-shoulder suit with silk linings that are some of the softest in the world. All of the work is done on the premises by tailors who have been with the firm for several decades. With advance notice a suit can be completed in three to four days. Otherwise figure four to six weeks.

For a number of years Knize maintained branch shops in New York and Palm Beach. Those stores closed several years ago but the experience taught the firm the value of ready-to-wear merchandise. Now Knize always has on hand a selection of beautifully made men's and women's suits. Its motto is that a fine ready-to-wear suit is better than a poor custom-made model. As three of the salesmen are tailors themselves, and as all alterations are done in the expert Knize workrooms, one can pretty well count on an excellently fitting garment. Indeed it probably will fit better than most custom-made suits. A Knize ready-to-wear suit in all wool worsted begins at $750.

In addition to suits Knize carries its own specially designed ties. All are silk-lined and bias-cut ($26–30). Its fine custom-made cotton shirts with handmade buttonholes are $100. Since 1930 Knize has even stocked its own brand of cologne and perfume.

This is certainly no place for a poor man to shop. But if you happen to be in Vienna in January or late July there is a storewide sale. Even with 20 percent off, though, these are hardly bargain goods for American dollars.

LANZ
KÄRNTNERSTRASSE 10
VIENNA, A-1010
522 456
MON.–FRI. 9–6, SAT. 9–12

Outside of Austria there is probably no clothing store better known than Lanz. For several decades now it has been almost the sole exporter of fine, high-quality traditional Austrian apparel. Of course what is sent abroad is only a small sampling of what can be found on the premises. There you will see a surprisingly broad selection of traditional costumes, sporting wear and updated Austrian-styled fashions, all made of sturdy, good quality fabrics and manufactured under the strictest specifications. These include dirndl dresses, loden suits, Salzburg jackets, lederhosen, loden coats, blouses, hats as well as a unique collection of accessories.

Many of these items are interesting as social artifacts. But unless you intend to spend a good deal of time in Austria participating in folk festivals, you would do better to merely browse, not buy. The exception to this rule is the traditionally styled Austrian outerwear. Loden coats for both men and women have become classics, which means you never have to worry about them going out of style. Those sold here for $300 are nearly indestructible. You can wear them a lifetime.

Lanz's main store is in Salzburg where the company began in 1928. They now have five branch stores. The Vienna store is devoted mostly to women's clothes but it does carry a fine selection of men's outerjackets and overcoats.

LODEN–PLANKL

MICHAELERPLATZ 6
VIENNA, A-1010
525 868
MON.–FRI. 9–6, SAT. 8:30–12:30

Loden–Plankl was founded almost 150 years ago and I am sure some of its extraordinary hunting clothes and outerwear is still in use. All fabrics for these garments are versions of loden cloth, which is made from a heavy wool yarn from the Tyrol region woven tightly and finished with a felt nap. This cloth is warm, waterproof and wears like a sheet of iron mail.

Of special interest in this fabric are the wonderful wool capes and hunting coats with an interesting open shoulder for shooting. These start at $150. For $170 there is the classic loden coat with stitched shoulders and an inverted pleat in the rear. The design is so clean and functional that one can count on its continued stylishness.

Loden–Plankl prides itself on the strength and utility of its garments. Its sweaters are knitted six sizes too large, then soaked in special baths until the wool has shrunk to the proper size. This makes the sweaters practically impermeable. They are as warm as jackets and yet have the flexibility of sweaters. Available in a number of different styles and color, these sweaters sell for $75 and up.

Also on hand are some wonderful knee-high wool socks at $20 a pair. Normally worn with traditional knickers, they are perfect under a pair of trousers for use on fall outings or for skiing or skating.

P. & C. HABIG

WIEDNER HAUPTSTRASSE 15
VIENNA
658 104
MON.–FRI. 9–6, SAT. 9–12

Without question P. & C. Habig is *the* hat shop of the world. Founded in 1860 by Peter Habig, this firm has custom-made hats for nearly all of Europe's royalty including Frederick William III, last king of Prussia, and King Edward VII of England.

Even if you never have worn a hat and never intend to, this shop is worth a visit. Entering through a pair of 15-foot-high doors, their polished wood frames surrounding the most delicately etched panes of glass, one can immediately feel the history and tradition of this century-old enterprise, begun at a time when the Hapsburgs were still in power. Filling the enormous first floor are ceiling-high columns of hats, eighteen different styles, each available in every conceivable size and in a wide selection of fabrics and colors. On top of these huge display cabinets are kept the royal orders, many going back to the middle of the nineteenth century.

In the rear of the store and on the floor above are the workshops. A hat can be custom-made there in a day, though usually Habig asks three to four weeks to fill an order.

Wool felt homburgs, either from stock or made-to-order, begin at $48. Habig's famous "Chapeau Claque," the collapsible top hat invented at the turn-of-the-century, is $85. For the ultimate in formal luxury try Habig's pure silk top hat, the only one still available in the world. For $140 you too can wear the hat of monarchs and statesmen.

8.
THE
FAR
EAST

Hong Kong

HONG KONG has gained a reputation as the clothes center of the Far East. However it is not a city in which one *shops* for clothes. Though it has branches of all the major designer boutiques—Valentino, Gucci, Cardin, etc.—you will find a much better selection of ready-to-wear suits and shirts in America or Europe. And probably at better prices.

What cannot be duplicated elsewhere at least at such low cost is the custom work. Whether it be shoes, shirts, pajamas or suits, there is nothing that can't be made well in Hong Kong at a fraction of European or American prices.

Yet one must be extremely careful in ordering any garment. Specific directions regarding the styling and detail work are a necessity. If you want or need help in designing your clothes, go to Savile Row. There can be no collaboration in Hong Kong. The tailors and cutters here simply have no sense of Western style and can be counted on to bollix any garment when left on their own. If, on the other hand, you know what you want and can say so, and appreciate fine handwork but can no longer afford Western prices, Hong Kong welcomes you with open arms.

ASCOT CHANG COMPANY

HOTEL PENINSULA
6, MEZZANINE FLOOR
KOWLOON, HONG KONG
K–662398
MON.–SAT. 9–7, SUN. 9–5

This firm is the most respected shirtmaker in Hong Kong. It is a respect that is well deserved. All its work is done by hand including the shirt buttonholes. There is single-needle stitching on each shirt seam.

In business over thirty years, Ascot Chang continues to service a worldwide clientele, many of whom send in their orders by mail. It makes shirts and prototype garments for almost all the European and American designers who come to work in Hong Kong.

Thomas Lain and Nelson Chin are the managers. They are the most experienced personnel in the shop as well as the most helpful. They can show you a selection of collars and cuffs to choose from though you are probably better off bringing a shirt to be copied. Unfortunately the cutter at Ascot Chang will not work from a drawing. If you have something special in mind—like a certain pocket or collar—bring a sample.

Shirts normally take three days to make. In cotton they are $25–27, in silk, $35–40.

Ascot Chang also makes elegant silk pajamas with fine embroidery. At $75 they are one of Hong Kong's great bargains.

H. BAROMON LTD.

23 CHARTER ROAD
HONG KONG
5–236 845; 5–233 238
MON.–SAT. 9–7

This is the largest and most famous tailoring shop in Hong Kong. The owner, Mr. Hoi, is at age eighty-five considered the dean of Hong Kong tailors. He has made suits for John F. Kennedy, Michael Todd and Edward G. Robinson, to name only a few of the celebrities who have sought out Baromon on their visits to the Far East. He continues to cut every suit made by the firm.

Originally begun in Shanghai, Baromon moved to Hong Kong thirty-two years ago. Most of the tailors moved with the shop and today the age of the workers averages more than sixty years old. This is a firm that believes in tradition. The suits they make have few local peers in terms of quality and workmanship. Only the finest wool fabrics are used and every piece is sewn by hand. Baromon takes a full week to do a suit.

The cost is high for Hong Kong, $450–750. Yet there is probably no suit made with more care. Mr. Hoi says, "If a customer is happy then I am." He truly means this. Making a fine suit is Mr. Hoi's great love.

Yet unfortunately there is a great separation between the kind of suits Mr. Hoi loves, and the type of suits men are wearing today. Perhaps because of his age and that of the other tailors, or perhaps because of the strength of their earlier Shanghai training, the only suit Baromon can turn out is a stodgy old man's suit, a Shanghai suit of the 1950's. This is a suit someone's grandfather might admire, but most men under fifty will probably not be so enamored.

LEE KUNG MAN KNITTING FACTORY
192-200 NAM CHEONG STREET
KOWLOON, HONG KONG
3 772 439
MON.–SAT. 9:30–7, OPEN ALTERNATE SUNDAYS

This shop is little more than a hole in the wall, and yet its clientele is practically a Who's Who in the fashion world. Basically Lee Kung makes underwear. But what brings those in the know to its door is the quality of its T-shirts, both cotton and wool.

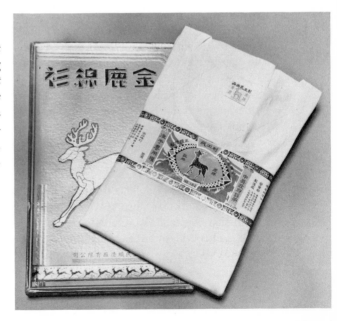

The finest cotton T-shirt in the world from Hong Kong. Available in short or long sleeves, these shirts are made from unbelievably strong 140-count pima cotton yarn, $8.50.

For $8.50 you can buy the finest all-cotton T-shirt in the world. The cloth is 140-count English yarn, about six times as dense a cotton weave as the normal commercial T-shirt. These shirts will hardly shrink in washing and are nearly indestructible, and their feel on the body is an absolute delight. Unfortunately the largest size Lee Kung makes is 42.

The other item of interest is the long-sleeved wool T-shirt, great for wear under a sportshirt in the winter or just by itself with a pair of jeans. These shirts are woven from the lightest English wool yarn and yet they are surprisingly durable. Their cost—a mere $17.

MAYLIN SHOE COMPANY
HOTEL PENINSULA
ME 3, MEZZANINE FLOOR
KOWLOON, HONG KONG
K-685 092
MON.–SAT. 9–7

This shop is a relative newcomer to the Hong Kong clothing scene. Begun only eight years ago, Maylin probably makes the finest quality shoe in the city. For $75–80 you can have a pair of shoes made to order that would be worth two or three times that price if purchased in Europe or the United States.

Yet do not be fooled by the apparent air of Western sophistication evinced by Maylin's salesmen. Like most firms in Hong Kong this is not a place to visit asking for advice. If you have a pair of favorite shoes you want duplicated there is no question that Maylin can do it well. But never leave a stylistic decision undecided. Instead demand that it follows your instructions exactly. Insist on the use of only the finest skins.

I remember the time a Texan ordered a pair of cowboy boots because his girlfriend had been satisfied with the copy Maylin had made of hers. But he had no boots to show. He accepted their assurances that the salesmen knew precisely what he had in mind. When he returned several days later what he found resembled less an American cowboy boot than some kind of Chinese pagoda on heels. These boots were so ludicrous looking they were actually almost interesting. The Texan, however, was not amused.

Do not be afraid to use Maylin. The manager, Jackson Li, knows his craft well. Just be certain you have a pair of shoes on hand to copy, or else give strict and complete instructions about a new style you've decided to try.

T. M. TOM

HOTEL PENINSULA
8, MEZZANINE FLOOR
KOWLOON, HONG KONG
K–663 968
MON.–SUN. 9–7

Like most of the fine tailors in Hong Kong, T. M. Tom began in Shanghai and left China after the war. He has been installed at the Peninsula Hotel since 1954. Suits are made here in three to four days and start at $225 for two-piece all wool.

This is a firm that specializes in high style. Suits are cut following the latest European fashions and are made from quality fabrics with considerable care. If you're looking to have a fitted Italian or French suit copied, Tom could probably pull it off as well as anyone in Hong Kong. This is not a tailor for the traditionalist but for someone seeking a designer look at Hong Kong prices.

YING TAI LURT

HOTEL PENINSULA
1A, MEZZANINE
KOWLOON, HONG KONG
K–667 242
MON.–SAT. 9:30–6:30, SUN. 9–2

This is a wonderful shop in which to have a suit made. Charlie Cheng, the general manager, is an old master at taking care of a customer in the grand manner. The service at Ying Tai is faultless. If you order some clothes, Charlie will likely offer to take you to his private antique shop where he will provide you with a special price on some rare merchandise. Or he might even take you to dinner at the Hong Kong Jockey Club.

Gordon Lau, the cutter, is patient, ingratiating and extremely competent. In four days you can have a completed all-wool suit that is made as well as almost any suit in the world. Prices start at $240 for two pieces. The problem here, as elsewhere in Hong Kong, is the styling. It cannot be a joint styling venture between you and the tailor. You must know precisely what you want. The best idea is to bring a garment with you to be copied or photographs that show specific detailing. Otherwise you must know how to direct the tailors so that there is no question about the size of the lapel, for example, or how much drape the coat should have.

A special bonus at Ying Tai is S.K. Mah, one of the finest women's tailors in the world. Mah's father was tailor to the last Emperor of China. Mah himself has been with Ying Tai for thirty years. If your wife or girlfriend orders something special, Mah might make it all by himself in the back room if he feels he is the only person able to execute it. Otherwise he will oversee all the steps ensuring an excellent fit and high-quality workmanship.

Ying Tai also has a branch in the Hilton Hotel.

Tokyo

THE BEST stores in Tokyo are those shaped by the single biggest influence on Japan—America. These firms look like small university shops that can be found throughout the United States, shops carrying tweed jackets, button-down shirts and penny loafers. Brooks Brothers recently opened a branch here and has been extremely successful. Paul Stuart preceded them by almost a year.

Unfortunately because of Japanese sizing most clothes sold in Tokyo do not fit Westerners. But even if they did one would do much better buying this traditional Ivy League merchandise from the original source. The selection is naturally wider in the United States and clothes are considerably cheaper. The Sperry topsider is $86 in Tokyo—almost two and a half times its price in the U.S. It sells like crazy.

Tokyo has its share of European imports and local designers as well. Italian and French suits, because of huge import duties, are very expensive. Clothing by local designers is more reasonable because it is manufactured within Japan. Much of it is quite interesting, a fusing of contemporary Western styles with Japanese detailing. Unfortunately many young Japanese designers go unnoticed in their own country until they become recognized in Europe and the United States. And while they are producing in Japan, their merchandise will not fit most Western bodies.

Still one should not miss shopping in Japan. The service is always impeccable, the Japanese do everything with great style, and it is fascinating to see our Western styles, particularly the Brooks Brothers look, worn by members of a culture so totally foreign to our own.

BERKELEY
4 30-6 Gingumae
Shibuya-ku, Tokyo
401–7185
Mon.–Sun. 12–8

Berkeley is ten years old and like most of the better quality men's stores in Tokyo carries the traditional American collegiate look. Its approach is similar to that of Teijin Men's Shop, though its market is somewhat younger. Like a university shop at Brooks Brothers or Saks Fifth Avenue, Berkeley directs its business toward the young man from age twenty to thirty. The sizing and fit of garments are Japanese but an American teenager visiting Tokyo might enjoy shopping here since he would probably fit into the clothes.

Berkeley is owned by the New Yorker manufacturing company, which in turn is owned by Daido, a conglomerate controlling 49 percent of Brooks Brothers in Japan. The merchandise of the two stores is complementary.

Berkeley carries oxford-cloth button-down shirts, $28–50, and cotton trousers in pink, yellow, blue and seersucker, $35–40. Khakis are $40 and knit polo-striped shirts, $25–30. Sportjackets in madras and seersucker are $150. In the winter there are wool flannel trousers, $50–60, and worsted suits, $175–250.

And what could be more collegiate American than a department selling blazer buttons? Berkeley has one. The sets, in silver or gold plate, are $20.

BROOKS BROTHERS
5-6 Kitaaoyama 3-chome
Minato-ku, Tokyo
404–4295
Mon.–Sun. 11–7, closed Wed.

This Brooks Brothers looks like any of the Brooks branch stores from Boston to San Francisco with one exception: the salesmen. They don't look like they attended Ivy League colleges though it's possible they might have. The shock for a Westerner entering this store is to see Brooks Brothers completely transplanted, only the American-dressed salesmen now have Oriental faces. But don't be intimidated. The salesmen here have as much knowledge of Brooks clothing as their counterparts in the States.

Much of the merchandise sold here comes directly from the firm's factories in the United States. Other items are manufactured in Japan under the parent company's direct supervision. The only difference in the clothes here is the size. You won't find any suits in 44, or even 42.

The best selling item in the store is the Brooks cotton lisle golf shirt at $45. Of course the Japanese love golf, and they walk about the store in their Brooks knit shirts, bright slacks and tassel loafers. The traditional Brooks oxford-cloth button-down shirt is $45 here; madras sportjackets are $450. The only garment exclusive to their branch is a Brooks Brothers sweatshirt offered in the oxford cloth colors of blue, pink and yellow. On the front is the Brooks golden fleece logo. At $30 the store can't keep enough in stock.

This Brooks Brothers branch opened only a year ago, but it is already turning a huge profit. As the father of American university wear, the style most favored by young successful Japanese, its future looks very bright.

EIKOKUYA
2 CHOME GINZA-DORI
CHUO-KU, TOKYO
563-2941
MON.–SUN. 10–7

Eikokuya is the most prestigious tailoring firm in Japan. It services the royal family as well as the country's past and present prime ministers. Such a clientele is used to luxury and gracious service, and surely in this regard Eikokuya does not disappoint. The shop has beautiful walnut paneling, chandeliers, a plush red rug with Eikokuya's name and motif woven into the design and handsome walnut chairs with striped velvet covers. In the fitting room a customer is provided with Christian Dior slippers to wear in order not to soil his feet while changing his trousers.

Eikokuya means "English store" in Japanese. The suits are modeled on old Savile Row designs and the only fabrics are fine English woolens. Many of these fabrics hang from 4-foot bolts displayed about the store.

Eikokuya was begun forty years ago by Mr. Kobayashi who confined the store's efforts then to the making of suits. Today Eikokuya also custommakes shirts of Swiss and English fabrics. Shirts cost $100–150 apiece and take a month to make. Suits begin at $1000 and require a three- to four-week delivery time. The suits are completely silk-lined and require only one fitting.

Eikokuya remains special to Tokyo. It is one of the few remaining shops still swearing obeisance to Japan's Old World respect for the English tradition.

THE GINZA
7 CHOME GINZA-4TH FLOOR
TOKYO
572–2121
MON.–SUN. 11–7

The Ginza is a relatively new high class department store with a menswear shop on the fourth floor. Owned by Shiseido, Japan's largest cosmetics manufacturer, this store offers a classy alternative to the traditional university look featured by so many of Tokyo's better shops. The Ginza sells high-styled Italian fashion.

The shop itself is of tasteful contemporary design, with glass and chrome fixtures mixed with Chinese lacquered appurtenances. It sells suits and jackets by Armani and Valentino, $650 and up, shoes by Rossetti, $150 and up, and shirts by Punch, the finest in Europe, $115–150.

The clothing sold here is "fashion" merchandise. It is high quality but trendy, thus potentially subject to quick obsolescence. However if you are looking for a quality selection of European fashion, this is the place in Tokyo.

PARCO BUILDING II
SHIBUYA-KU AREA
TOKYO
MON.–SUN. 11–8

If you want to see a good selection of contemporary Japanese design, this is the place to go. Parco Building II is part of a series of very modern Tokyo department stores that, like Bloomingdale's in New York, is divided into small hip boutiques on each floor. The basement floor carries the best of the Japanese designers such as Issey Miyake and Takeo Kikuchi in boutiques called Men's Bigi and Garcon.

These small shops are stark modern areas fitted out with glass and chrome fixtures, white counters and marble floors. They attract a purely younger crowd, "chic Tokyo," that group of well-traveled, sophisticated, upper-middle-class Japanese.

The clothing here is Western in orientation, jeans, unusually knit sweaters, suits and jackets in modish styles. The look is young and trendy but generally the clothing is tastefully chosen and of legitimately good design.

Prices are not high by Japanese standards—trousers $50, shirts $30–40, jackets and suits $100–250 and imported shoes $150–200.

These stores are always interesting to visit and occasionally you will find an item of great long term design. The problem for a Westerner, in this case, will be to find the garment in his size.

TEIJIN MEN'S SHOP
4.3.10 GINZA, CHUO-KU
TOKYO
561-7519
MON.–SUN. 11:30–8

This shop is one of twenty Teijin stores in Tokyo and Osaka that have been opened since 1960 by the Teijin Corporation, a giant fabric mill. It is the original shop and remains the chain's flagship. For someone seeking updated traditional merchandise it is probably the nicest store in Tokyo in which to shop. The merchandise is of first-rate quality and attractively displayed. The salesmen are knowledgeable, well dressed and act as if they truly enjoy their work.

Curiously the Teijin Men's Shop was begun merely as a showroom to display the company's newest cloth, most of which was polyester. Yet so successful did the store become that Teijin quickly changed its mind about its purposes. Today very little of what the shop carries is made of man-made fibers. Indeed looking about one sees only linens, cotton twills and wool blends.

The dominant fashion in Japan at the time Teijin opened was the American Ivy League look of the 1950's. Teijin chose that look, which it continues to show today, and reflected it in the style of the store as well. There are brick floors and wood paneling on the store's two levels. Clothing is displayed in highly polished pine cabinets and on the walls are hung Spy prints and English horseman motifs in brass. The salesmen dress in suspenders and wear pin-collar shirts with rep ties, khakis and tassel loafers. Suits are the store's main business and they are sold on the basement floor. Teijin's own wool suits, natural-shoulder models with a bit of shape, start at $250. But it also carries Ralph Lauren and Sal Cesarini. All suits are Japanese-sized.

Upstairs on the main floor are the traditional furnishings, a fine selection of rep and foulard ties, $20–30; small bow ties in unusual silks such as a pink paisley; and shoes from England and the United States. The tassel loafer is $135; Sperry topsiders are $86. John Smedley cotton lisle shirts are $60; and for $9 you can buy tartan plaid sleeve bands to hold up shirt sleeves that are too long.

Teijin also carries an interesting sprinkling of nonapparel merchandise: Kent tooth and hair brushes, leather toiletry kits and shaving mugs, wicker picnic baskets and extremely beautiful shoulder bags by Hunting World, $450, made in Japan but meeting Hunting World's traditionally demanding standards.

This is an exceptionally fine shop. Each season it produces a beautiful full-color catalog that manages to capture the store's full breadth of elegance and style.